Preface

You are my Grammar & Speaking series is a basic grammar book for beginner learners. There are 61 units in series and each unit is about a different point of English grammar. With the various exercises, interesting photos, and illustrations, students will enjoy English grammar and really can communicate in English, even from the beginning. This book encourages students to speak and write English accurately and fluently by providing them with a solid understanding of English grammar.

This book uses a simple but systematic 4-step approach (Real-life Context, Learn & Practice, Super Writing, Super Speaking) to help young learners master English grammar. This series aims to motivate young learners to learn grammar through various creative tasks such as Super Writing, Super Speaking, and various levels of challenging questions.

You are my Grammar & Speaking series is a useful supplement to any English language courses and is suitable for both classroom teaching and self-study. The series focuses on the key grammar concepts that students need to know for written exercises.

I hope many students will build language and communication skills with this *You are my Grammar & Speaking series*. At the same time, I wish teachers will use *You are my Grammar & Speaking series* as the most appropriate tool for teaching English as a second language. If students learn one language well, they will be able to learn other languages easily. That is why grammar is necessary to learn languages.

I am convinced that through this *You are my Grammar & Speaking series*, a lot of students will definitely have the chance to improve and develop their English grammar skills and abilities.

Thanks and good luck,

Lucifer EX

Structure & Features

You are my Grammar & Speaking series is an easy, friendly, and interesting grammar book series designed for young learners. The series contains interesting photos and illustrations to help students understand grammar points. With this grammar book series, the leaners will learn the rules of essential English grammar with the information about when and how to use them.

• Step 1: *Real-life Context*

The purpose of this part is to introduce students to the grammar point of the unit. This helps students to start the lesson in a very meaningful real-life context with captivating images.

• Step 2: *Learn & Practice*

Vivid photos and illustrations stimulate students' interest and help them understand the meaning and use of grammar. Clear and easy-to-read grammar charts present the grammar structure. The accompanying examples ensure that students understand the grammar point with colorful photos and illustrations.

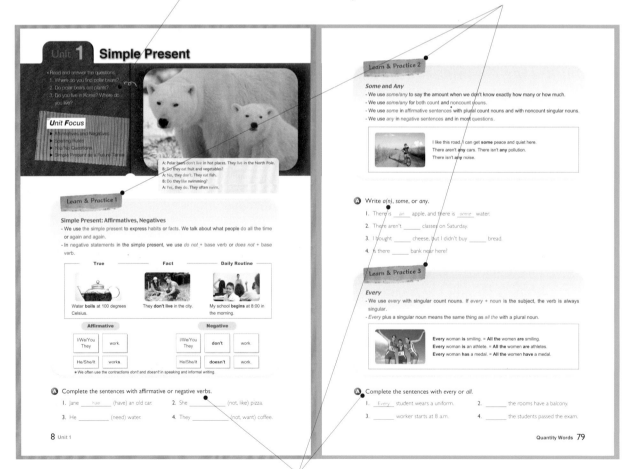

Each Learn & Practice *provides various basic exercises and opportunities to practice both the forms and the uses of the grammar structure.*

You are my
Grammar &
Speaking

2 Student Book

Iam books

Published by

I am Books

#1116, Daeryung Techno Town 12th Bldg.,

14, Gasan digital 2-ro, Geumcheon-gu, Seoul 153-778, Republic of Korea

TEL: 82-2-6343-0999

FAX: 82-2-6343-0995

Visit our website: http://www.iambooks.co.kr

Publishers: Shin Sunghyun, Oh Sangwook

Author: Lucifer EX

Editor: Kim Hyeona

Photo Credits:

Wikipedia (www.wikipedia.org): p. 28 (Marilyn Monroe); p. 31 (Lee Byunghun) ⓒ Eva Rinaldi; p. 31 (Hugh Jackman) ⓒ Eva Rinaldi; p. 31 (Kate Winslet) ⓒ Andrea Raffin; p. 31 (Jackie Chan) ⓒ Gage Skidmore; p. 34 (Mona Lisa); p. 38 (traditional sled, qamutik) ⓒ Ansgar Walk; p. 38 (Inuk in a kayak) ⓒ Edward S. Curtis; p. 38 (Fashionable Ladies of the Day); p. 40 (Cristiano Ronaldo); p. 72 (British versions of the Harry Potter series) ⓒ Mo HH92 (Original uploader at en.wikipedia); p. 112 (J. K. Rowling) ⓒ Daniel Ogren; p. 134 (CIA World Factbook Political World Map)

All other photos ⓒ Imagetoday (www.imagetoday.co.kr)

ISBN: 978-89-6398-093-5 63740

• Step 3: *Super Writing*

A writing activity allows students to interact with one another and further develop their speaking and writing skills. Through these activities, students will have a chance to apply their understanding of the practical uses of grammar.

• Step 4: *Super Speaking*

Super Speaking offers students rich opportunities to apply newly learned grammar to speaking activities. This section will help students to develop speaking skills. Students work in pairs or groups and perform a variety of real-life tasks, progressing smoothly from controlled to free practice. By doing so, the amount of time students speak is increased significantly and cooperation among students is encouraged. In addition, pair and group works help students lessen their communicative stress because it is easier for them to communicate with their peers rather than their teachers.

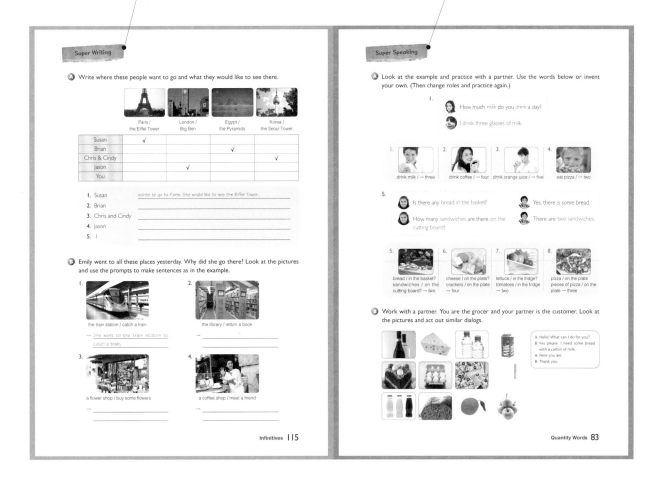

Contents

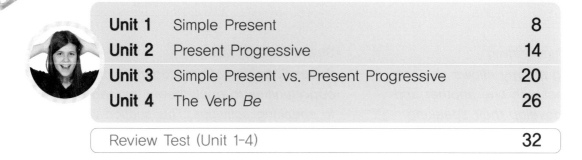

You are my
Grammar &
Speaking

2 Student Book

 books

Simple Present

- Read and answer the questions.
1. Where do you find polar bears?
2. Do polar bears eat plants?
3. Do you live in Korea? Where do you live?

Unit Focus

▶ Affirmatives and Negatives
▶ Spelling Rules
▶ Yes/No Questions
▶ Simple Present as a Future Tense

A: Polar bears don't live in hot places. They live in the North Pole.
B: Do they eat fruit and vegetables?
A: No, they don't. They eat fish.
B: Do they like swimming?
A: Yes, they do. They often swim.

Learn & Practice 1

Simple Present: Affirmatives, Negatives

- We use the simple present to express habits or facts. We talk about what people do all the time or again and again.
- In negative statements in the simple present, we use *do not* + base verb or *does not* + base verb.

True	Fact	Daily Routine
Water **boils** at 100 degrees Celsius.	They **don't live** in the city.	My school **begins** at 8:00 in the morning.

Affirmative

I/We/You They	work.
He/She/It	works.

Negative

I/We/You They	**don't**	work.
He/She/It	**doesn't**	work.

＊We often use the contractions *don't* and *doesn't* in speaking and informal writing.

A Complete the sentences with affirmative or negative verbs.

1. Jane _____has_____ (have) an old car.

2. She _____ (not, like) pizza.

3. He _____ (need) water.

4. They _____ (not, want) coffee.

Simple Present: Spelling Rules of Final *-s* and *-es*

- We add *-s* or *-es* to the verb to make the third person singular (he/she/it).

Olivia **lives** in Korea.
She **plays** tennis in the morning.
She **does** her homework in the afternoon.
She **sits** in front of the television in the evening.
She **drinks** milk and **watches** her favorite program.

-s	work → work**s** eat → eat**s** open → open**s** write → write**s**	• Most verbs take **-s** in the third-person singular.
-es	watch → watch**es** wash → wash**es** fix → fix**es** go → go**es** pass → pass**es**	• Verbs ending in **-ss**, **-sh**, **-ch**, **-x** and **-o** take **-es**.
-ies	study → stud**ies** fly → fl**ies** worry → worr**ies**	• Verbs ending in a **consonant + -y**, drop the **-y** and take **-ies**
-s	play → play**s** stay → stay**s** buy → buy**s**	• Verbs ending in **vowel + -y**, take **-s**.
Irregular	have → **has**	• No rules

Ⓐ Write the third person singular form of the verbs.

1. live → _lives_

2. speak → _____

3. push → _____

4. cry → _____

5. stay → _____

6. buy → _____

7. make → _____

8. do → _____

9. have → _____

Ⓑ Write the third person singular form of the verbs in brackets.

1. He _wears_ (wear) a suit to work.

2. Sunny _____ (get up) at 7:00.

3. She _____ (go) to school.

4. He _____ (read) newspapers on the train.

5. He _____ (hurry) to work in the morning.

6. She _____ (play) soccer on Saturday mornings.

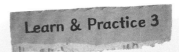

Simple Present: *Yes/No* Questions

- We use *do* or *does* to make questions in the simple present. Use *do* with *I, you, we*, and *they*. Use *does* with *he, she*, and *it*.

——— Statements ———	——— Questions ———
He plays the guitar.	Q: **Does** he play the guitar?
	A: Yes, he **does**.
She wears glasses.	Q: **Does** she wear glasses?
	A: No, she **doesn't**.
They like K-pop music.	Q: **Do** they like K-pop music?
	A: Yes, they **do**.

(A) Make *yes/no* questions and complete the short answers.

1. He has a smartphone. → Q: Does he have a smartphone? _____ A: Yes, he does _____ .

2. She knows his family. → Q: _____ A: No, _____ .

3. They need more money. → Q: _____ A: Yes, _____ .

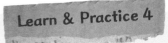

Simple Present as a Future Tense

- The simple present is used for events that are part of a timetable or schedule. While the events are in the future, their existence is already established in the present, so we use the simple present.

Q: What time **does** the baseball game **begin** tomorrow?
A: It **begins** at 6:00 tomorrow.

(A) Circle the correct words and check the correct meanings.

1. A chicken (come / comes) from an egg. Future: _____ / Fact: ___✓___

2. The train (arrive / arrives) at 8:00 this evening. Future: _____ / Habit: _____

3. When does class (begins / begin) tomorrow? Future: _____ / Fact: _____

4. Lisa (don't / doesn't) drink coffee in the morning. Future: _____ / Habit: _____

A Make questions using the prompts given. Then, answer them in the negative form.

1. Bob / work / at a restaurant

   Q: *Does Bob work at a restaurant?*   A: No, he doesn't.

2. Ava / exercise / every morning

   Q: _____   A: _____

3. Jane's taxi / go / to the subway station

   Q: _____   A: _____

4. Tom / always / study / at home / in the evening

   Q: _____   A: _____

5. the bus / come / every ten minutes

   Q: _____   A: _____

B Write two sentences about each picture.

1. I don't watch TV.
   I study Korean every day.

   → Kelly *doesn't watch TV. She studies Korean every day*

2. I don't teach French.
   I teach English.

   → The teacher _____

3. I don't have a cat.
   I have a puppy.

   → Amy _____

4. I don't play basketball on Tuesday afternoons.
   I play tennis on Tuesday afternoons.

   → Luke _____

   _____

Simple Present 11

C Use the prompts to complete the sentences as in the example.

1.

begin / at 2:00 / tomorrow

→ The concert *begins at 2:00 tomorrow* .

2.

leave / at 7:00 / tonight

→ My plane _____ .

3.

the laundry shop / open / tomorrow

→ What time _____

_____ ?

4.

leave / at 6:00 p.m. / tomorrow

→ The next train to New York _____

_____ .

D What do the students do *in the evenings* after school? Ask and answer, as in the example.

1.

Chris / watch a DVD
→ No / listen to music

Q: *Does Chris watch a DVD in the evenings?*

A: *No, he doesn't. He listens to music.*

2.

Lisa / play on the computer
→ No / read books

Q: _____

A: _____

3.

Rachel / take exercise
→ No / have an English lesson

Q: _____

A: _____

4.

John / ride a bicycle
→ No / ride a skateboard

Q: _____

A: _____

A Look at the example and practice with a partner. Use the words below or invent your own. (Repeat 3 times.)

1.

Tom / live in an apartment?

1.

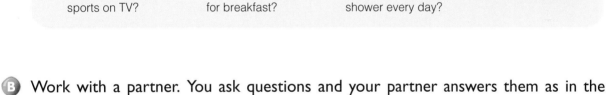

Does Tom live in an apartment?

No, he doesn't. Do you live in an apartment?

Yes, I live in an apartment.

2. Bruce / enjoy sports on TV?

3. Kelly / eat fast food for breakfast?

4. Betty / have a shower every day?

5. Mark / like vegetables?

B Work with a partner. You ask questions and your partner answers them as in the example. Then change roles.

1. like / coffee?
2. like / math?
3. have / a cell phone?
4. like / vegetables?
5. walk / to school / every day?
6. listen to / K-pop music?
7. often / go / to the park?
8. read / newspapers / every day?
9. play / soccer?
10. often / go / to movie theaters?
11. speak / English/Korean?
12. swim / in summer?

Do you like coffee?
Do you have a cell phone?

No, I don't.
I like green tea.
Yes, I do.

Your turn to ask.

How well do you know your partner?

I know my partner really well. She likes green tea and she has a cell phone. _____

_____

_____

_____

Present Progressive

• Read and answer the questions.
1. What is Olivia doing now?
2. Is she smiling?
3. Is she wearing sneakers?
4. What are you doing now?

Unit Focus

▶ Affirmatives and Negatives
▶ Spelling Rules of Verb-*ing*
▶ Yes/No Questions

Olivia **isn't working** today.
She's on holiday.

Peter: Hi, Olivia! Where are you?
Olivia: I'm in Paris. I'm visiting the Eiffel
Tower. I'm taking pictures of the city.
What are you doing now?
Peter: I'm studying for my Korean exams now.
Olivia: Oh!!!

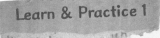
Learn & Practice 1

Present Progressive: Affirmatives, Negatives

- We use the present progressive to talk about actions happening right now, at the moment of speaking.
- We use the present progressive for temporary actions happening around now, but not at the actual moment of speaking.
- We form the present progressive with the present tense of the verb *be* and the base verb with the ending -*ing*. (*be* + base verb-*ing*)

Right Now	**Around Now**

Oh, Cindy! Can I call you later? **I'm driving** now.	I want to buy a new smartphone, so **I'm working** part-time at a restaurant this month. (Right now she is not working. She is walking.)

- To make the negative of the present progressive, we put *not* after the verb *be*.

Kathy **isn't standing** up.   Tom **isn't watching** TV.
She is sitting down.   He is talking on the phone.

Negative

am			
is	+	**not**	+	-ing
are			

A Complete the sentences using the present progressive and check.

1. She ____is making____ (make) spaghetti.   Right Now: __√__ / Around Now: ____

2. I _____ (take) piano lessons these days.   Right Now: ____ / Around Now: ____

3. He _____ (study) Japanese this semester.
                                                      Right Now: ____ / Around Now: ____

4. It _____ (snow) outside now.   Right Now: ____ / Around Now: ____

5. They _____ (listen) to the radio.   Right Now: ____ / Around Now: ____

Learn & Practice 2

Present Progressive: Spelling Rules of Verb-*ing*

go → going walk → walking study → studying eat → eating	• Add **-ing** to most verbs.
come → coming live → living make → making dance → dancing	• If a verb ends in a vowel + consonant + **-e**, remove **-e** and add **-ing**.
swim → swimming sit → sitting run → running get → getting	• if a verb ends in a vowel + consonant, **double the consonant** and add **-ing**.

∗ Exception: verbs that end in *w, x, y*. Do not double the last consonant.

show → show**ing**, fix → fix**ing**, say → say**ing**

A Fill in the blanks with the verbs in the present progressive.

1.   look   People ____are looking____ at the clock.

2.   enjoy   The reporter _____ the evening.

3.   sit   I _____ in front of the window now.

4.   eat   A little girl _____ ice cream.

5.   study   She _____ Greek this semester.

6.   wear   The girls _____ jeans.

Present Progressive: *Yes/No* Questions

- In a *yes/no* question, we put *am*, *is*, or *are* before the subject.

Q: **Are** the children watching a movie**?**
A: **Yes**, they **are**.

Q: **Is** Lucas doing his homework**?**
A: **No**, he **isn't**. He's speaking on the phone.

- We often use short answers in speaking and informal writing. Don't use contractions in affirmative short answers.

Be Verb	Subject	Verb + *-ing*	
Am	I		**Yes**, I **am**. / **No**, I'm **not**.
Is	he/she/it/Bob, etc.	work**ing?**	**Yes**, she **is**. / **No**, she **isn't**.
Are	you/we/they		**Yes**, they **are**. / **No**, they **aren't**.

Ⓐ Write questions and short answers as in the example.

1. Jessica / cook chicken   (Yes)
   Q: _____ Is Jessica cooking chicken? _____   A: _____ Yes, she is. _____

2. the girl / wear a hat   (No)
   Q: _____   A: _____

3. Peter / play a computer game   (Yes)
   Q: _____   A: _____

4. you / write a letter   (No)
   Q: _____   A: _____

5. the dog / sit on the chair   (Yes)
   Q: _____   A: _____

6. they / celebrate their anniversary   (No)
   Q: _____   A: _____

A Look at the pictures. Use the prompts to make questions and answers to describe each picture, as in the example.

1.

he / paint / the car?
→ No / the wall

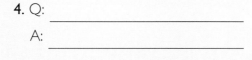

1. Q: Is he painting the car?
   A: No, he isn't. He is painting the wall.

2. Q: _____
   A: _____

3. Q: _____
   A: _____
   _____

4. Q: _____
   A: _____
   _____

2.

she / sit?
→ No / walk

3.

the girl / read / a magazine?
→ No / a book

4.

they / watch / TV?
→ No / see a movie

B Write questions and negations as in the example.

1. She's riding a bicycle.

Is she riding a bicycle?

She isn't riding a bicycle.

2. He's watching a horror movie.

_____

_____

3. You're talking on your mobile phone.

_____

_____

4. We're playing basketball.

_____

_____

5. They're wearing suits.

_____

_____

6. I am doing the right exercise.

_____

_____

C Look at the picture. Ask and answer questions as in the example.

1. (the girl / wear pants)

   Q: Is the girl wearing pants?

   A: Yes, she is.

2. (the mother / wear a white dress)

   Q: _____

   A: _____

3. (the mother and father / hold hands)

   Q: _____

   A: _____

4. (the mother and father / wear hats)

   Q: _____

   A: _____

5. (the people / stand)

   Q: _____

   A: _____

6. (the father / hold his son)

   Q: _____

   A: _____

D Look at the pictures and use the words or phrases in the box to correct the sentences.

skateboard	fly a kite	eat an ice cream

1.

Ava is doing her homework.

→ No, she isn't doing her homework. She is eating an ice cream.

2.

Kevin is riding a bicycle.

→ _____

_____

_____

3.

Jane is windsurfing.

→ _____

_____

_____

Ⓐ Look at the example and practice with a partner. Use the words below or invent your own. (Repeat 3 times.)

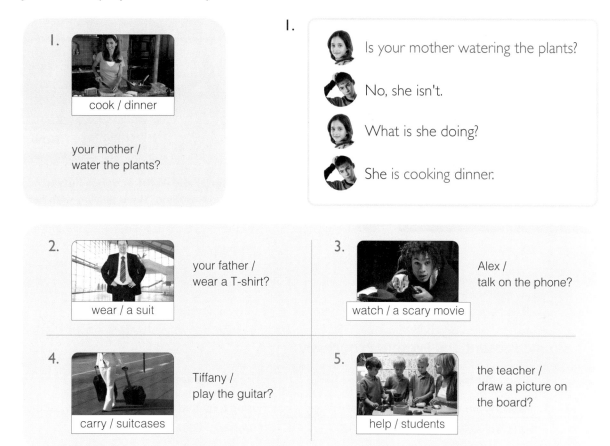

1.

1. cook / dinner	

your mother /
water the plants?

I.

Is your mother watering the plants?

No, she isn't.

What is she doing?

She is cooking dinner.

2. wear / a suit

your father /
wear a T-shirt?

3. watch / a scary movie

Alex /
talk on the phone?

4. carry / suitcases

Tiffany /
play the guitar?

5. help / students

the teacher /
draw a picture on
the board?

Ⓑ Talk in pairs. Student A chooses a picture from the ones below. Student B asks questions to find out who he/she is.

Lisa Steve Bob

Helen Olivia William

Susan Scott Jessica

Is it a man or a woman?
Is she swimming?
Is she playing the guitar?
Is she Lisa?

It's a woman.
No, she isn't.
Yes, she is.
Yes, she is.

Your turn to ask now!

• Read and answer the questions.
1. What do the people in the first picture usually do?
2. What is Sophia doing right now?
3. What are you doing tomorrow evening?

Unit Focus

▶ Meaning & Uses of Simple Present and Present Progressive
▶ *Always* + Present Progressive
▶ Present Progressive as a Future Tense

Usually　　　**Now**

Sophia **lives** in Los Angeles and **works** as a yoga instructor. It's Sunday now and she **isn't working**. She **is playing** with her children in the park.

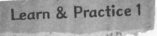

Learn & Practice 1

Simple Present and Present Progressive

Simple Present	Present Progressive
- For actions we do every day or actions which are repeated regularly E.g. We **go** to school every day. - For permanent states or facts E.g. He **lives** in London. 　　Water **boils** at 100 degrees Celsius.	- For actions that are happening now, at the moment of speaking E.g. She **isn't playing** the guitar right now. - For actions that are happening temporarily at the present period of time (but not exactly now, at the moment of speaking) E.g. I'm **working** in London this week.
Time Expressions	**(Time) Expressions**
every morning/day/week/year, etc. on Monday/Tuesday, etc. in the morning/afternoon/evening always, never, sometimes, often, etc.	now, at the moment, at present, these days, this week/month/year, today, etc. Look!, Listen!

My father is an athlete.
He **swims** 5 kilometers every day.
In this picture he **is swimming** in the pool.

My mother is an artist.
She always **draws** beautifully.
In this picture she **is drawing** some flowers.

A Circle the correct verb forms.

1. The sun is ((shining)/ shines) today.

2. She (living / lives) in Seoul.

3. Listen! The birds are (sing / singing).

4. He is (helps / helping) her at home these days.

5. I usually (take / taking) the school bus.

6. They are (sitting / sit) in class right now.

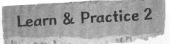

Always + Present Progressive

- We use the adverbs of frequency with the simple present. They show us how often something happens.

- The present progressive uses the adverb 'always' to express a habitual negative action.

Gyubin **always brushes** her teeth twice a day.

Don't lie. You **are always telling** lies. (to complain or to express annoyance)

- Frequency adverbs go before the main verb, but they go after the verb *be* and auxiliary verbs.
  - I'm **always** happy to be with her.
  - She can **always** listen to music.
  - They **never** drink coffee.
  - Paul doesn't **usually** eat out on Sundays.
  - He **rarely** goes to the movie theater.

Adverbs of Frequency	
always	100%
usually	75%
often	50%
sometimes	25%
seldom/rarely	10%
never	0%

A Circle the correct words and check.

1. The girl always ((wears)/ wearing) a smile.   Fact: __✓__ Complaint: ____

2. You're always (listen / listening) to music.   Habit: ____ Complaint: ____

3. He's never satisfied. He's always (complaining / complain).   Fact: ____ Complaint: ____

4. Kathy always (eats / eating) breakfast.   Habit: ____ Complaint: ____

Present Progressive as a Future Tense

- We use the present progressive to talk about future arrangements and plans. We often use a time expression with the present progressive.
- We use the present progressive especially with verbs of movement and transportation such as come, go, leave, fly, and travel.

Now	Prediction	Future Plan
They **are having** dinner right now.	Donna **will be** a great violinist one day.	Karen **is meeting** her friend in an hour.

- However, we cannot use the present progressive for future predictions.

A Complete the sentences using *will* or *be -ing* and check.

1. Sarah ___is flying___ (fly) to Singapore in two hours. Prediction: _____ Future Plan: _√_

2. Most people _____ (drive) electric cars. Prediction: _____ Now: _____

3. She _____ (study) French these days. Now: _____ Prediction: _____

4. A: What are you doing tonight?
   B: I _____ (see) a movie with my family. Now: _____ Future Plan: ____

5. People _____ (go) on vacation to the moon. Future Plan: _____ Prediction: _____

B Look and complete the sentences using the present progressive.

What are they doing this Saturday?

1.
   play / tennis

2.
   work / in her office

3.
   go / to the concert

Cindy ___is playing tennis___. Jessica _____. Bob and Amy _____
_____.

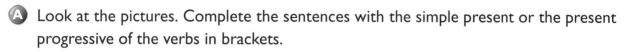
Super Writing

A Look at the pictures. Complete the sentences with the simple present or the present progressive of the verbs in brackets.

1.

Kathy usually ___drinks___ (drink) lemonade, but she ___is drinking___ (drink) orange juice now.

2.

I _____ (not work) on Saturdays, but I _____ (work) two Saturdays this month.

3.

Larry and Martha usually _____ (walk) in the park, but today they _____ (ride) their bicycles.

4.

This is my friend Tom. He is very good at tennis. He _____ (play) tennis on Saturday afternoons. In this picture, he _____ (play) tennis with his grilfriend.

B Look at the pictures as prompts. Read the questions and answer them using the simple present or the present progressive.

1.

clean / the room

Q: What is she doing?
A: _She is cleaning the room._____

2.

watch / TV

Q: What does Olivia do in the evening?
A: _____

3.

wear / a scarf

Q: What is Ava wearing?
A: _____

4.

drink / orange juice

Q: What does your brother have for breakfast?
A: _____

C Look at Jane's schedule and write about what she is doing on Monday. Use the present progressive.

> **MONDAY**
>
> 9:00   Arrive in Seoul.
>
> 10:00   Meet Bob and Tom.
>
> 12:00-2:00 Have lunch with Ava.
>
> 7:00   Wait for Kevin in the hotel lobby. Go for dinner.
>
> 11:00   Return to the hotel. Prepare for a meeting on Tuesday at 9:00.

1. What time is Jane arriving in Seoul?

   → She is arriving in Seoul at 9:00. _____

2. Who is she meeting at 10:00?

   → _____

3. What is she doing between 12:00 and 2:00?

   → _____

4. Where is she waiting for Kevin?

   → _____

5. What is she doing at 11:00?

   → _____

   _____

D Complete the sentences. Use *always* and the present progressive.

1. A: I'm afraid I've lost my smartphone.

   B: Not again! You _____ are always losing your smartphone _____ .

2. A: The radio has broken down again.

   B: That radio is a pain. It _____ .

3. A: Look! You made the same mistake again.

   B: Oh no, not again! I _____ .

4. A: Oh, I forgot my books again.

   B: That's typical! You _____ .

A Look at the example and practice with a partner. Use the words below or invent your own. (Repeat 3 times.)

1.

1.

Richard

Usually — read / a book

Now — wash / the dishes

What does Richard in the picture do in the evenings?

He usually reads a book. What's he doing now?

He is washing the dishes.

2.

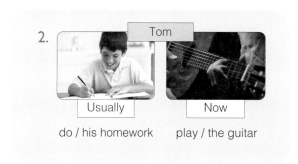

Tom

Usually — do / his homework

Now — play / the guitar

3.

Jessica

Usually — listen to / classical music

Now — watch / TV

B Work with a partner. Look at picture A and say what they usually do on Saturday mornings, as in the example. Then, look at picture B and say what they are doing this Saturday morning.

A. Every Saturday

Olivia

Mary Tom

William

B. This Saturday

Does William read a newspaper every Saturday morning?
Is he taking pictures now?

Yes, he does.
Yes, he is.

Your turn to ask!

Simple Present vs. Present Progressive 25

Unit 4 · The Verb *Be*

• Read and answer the questions.
1. Is Korea a beautiful and fascinating place?
2. How many bridges are there across the Han River?
3. Does the World Cup take place every four years?
4. Where were you yesterday afternoon?

Unit Focus

▶ The Verb *Be*: Affirmatives
▶ The Verb *Be*: Negatives
▶ The Verb *Be*: Yes/No Questions

Korea is a beautiful and fascinating place. Korea has a long history. Seoul is the capital of Korea. Across the Han River there are about twenty bridges. The subway will take you anywhere you need to go. The 1986 Asian Games and the 1988 Olympic Games were held in Seoul. In 2002, the FIFA World Cup was held in Korea and Japan. Korea placed 4th in the 2002 World Cup.

Learn & Practice 1

Present and Past of *Be*: Affirmatives

- There are three forms of present tense of *be*: am, is, and are.
- The simple past of the verb *be* has two forms: was and were.

Past	Now
We **were** beautiful *30 years ago*.	We **are** old now.

Present		Past	
I	am	I	was
he/she/it Tom/the dog, etc.	is	he/she/it Tom/the dog, etc.	was
you/we/they children/books, etc.	are	you/we/they children/books, etc.	were

She **is** a student, and he **is** a student too.
They **are** students.

Kathy **was** in Seoul last week.
We **were** in Seattle last year.

A Complete the sentences with *am*, *is*, *are*, *was*, or *were*.

1. They ___were___ in Europe two weeks ago.

2. Beethoven _____ born in 1770 in Germany.

3. I _____ an elementary school student now.

4. It _____ very humid today.

5. I have three books. They _____ on my desk.

6. Amy and Tom _____ in their offices yesterday.

Learn & Practice 2

Present and Past of *Be*: Negatives

- To make a negative statement, we put *not* after *be*: is (was) not / are (were) not.

He **isn't** a football player. He **is** a baseball player.	I **wasn't** a nurse 10 years ago. I **was** a doctor.	They **weren't** at home yesterday. They **were** at the birthday party.

Negative

Pronouns	Be	Not	Contractions
I	am/was		I'm not / wasn't
you	are/were		you **aren't/weren't**
he/she/it/Tom	is/was	not	he/she/it **isn't/wasn't**
we/they Tom and Jane	are/were		we/they **aren't/weren't**

A Rewrite the sentences in the negative. Use subject pronouns.

1. David and I are young. → *We aren't young.*

2. Kathy was late for school. → _____

3. My mom and dad were in the park. → _____

4. Peter is at the library today. → _____

5. Napoleon was a musician. → _____

Present and Past of *Be*: *Yes/No* Questions

- To make a question, we put the verb *be* before the subject. *Yes/No* questions end with a question mark (?).

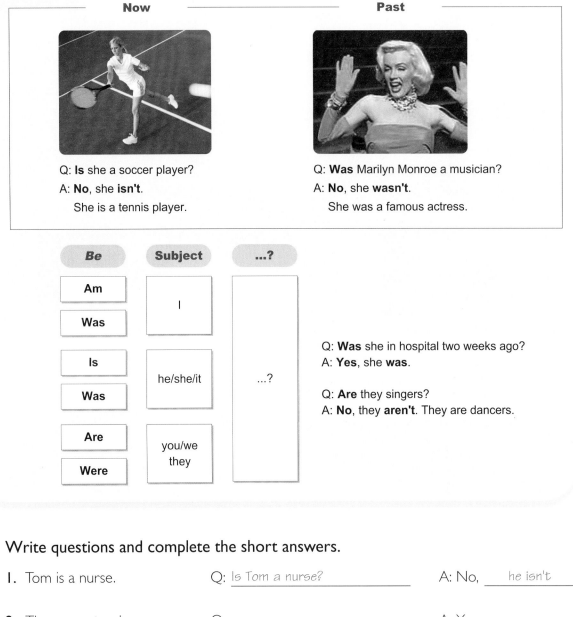

Now

Q: **Is** she a soccer player?
A: **No**, she **isn't**.
She is a tennis player.

Past

Q: **Was** Marilyn Monroe a musician?
A: **No**, she **wasn't**.
She was a famous actress.

Be	Subject	...?
Am		
Was	I	
Is		...?
Was	he/she/it	
Are		
Were	you/we they	

Q: **Was** she in hospital two weeks ago?
A: **Yes**, she **was**.

Q: **Are** they singers?
A: **No**, they **aren't**. They are dancers.

Ⓐ Write questions and complete the short answers.

1. Tom is a nurse.

Q: Is Tom a nurse?   A: No, _____he isn't_____.

2. They were teachers.

Q: _____ A: Yes, _____.

3. Angelina Joli is American.

Q: _____ A: Yes, _____.

4. Cindy is at home.

Q: _____ A: No, _____.

5. He was in the museum.

Q: _____ A: No, _____.

6. The girls were late for school.

Q: _____ A: Yes, _____.

Ⓐ Choose and complete the sentences using *is*, *are*, *was*, or *were*.

> an American businessman the capital of Korea Japanese cities
> my favorite subjects very good at the Chinese martial art, kung fu
> a painter famous painters

1. Tokyo and Nagoya _____*are Japanese cities*_____ .

2. Bill Gates _____ .

3. Seoul _____ .

4. English and biology _____ .

5. Jackie Chan _____ .

6. Leonardo da Vinci _____ .

4. Leonardo da Vinci and Michelangelo _____ .

Ⓑ Look at the pictures and prompts. Complete the questions and answer them.

> the airport a restaurant the shopping center the movie theater

1.

Ava / last night?

Q: Where ____*was Ava last night*____ ?

A: ____*She was at the movie theater.*____

2.

Susan / yesterday afternoon?

Q: Where _____ ?

A: _____

3.

Bob and Jane / now?

Q: Where _____ ?

A: _____

4.

they / now?

Q: Where _____ ?

A: _____

C Read the statements, then make questions and give short answers, as in the example.

1. Q: Is Tom here today?

   A: No, he isn't.   (Tom isn't here today.)

2. Q: _____

   A: _____ (Nancy wasn't busy yesterday.)

3. Q: _____

   A: _____ (Steve isn't a basketball player.)

4. Q: _____

   A: _____ (Sunny and Isabel weren't bakers 10 years ago.)

5. Q: _____

   A: _____ (My sisters aren't elementary school students.)

6. Q: _____

   A: _____ (Kelly wasn't at home yesterday.)

D Look at the pictures. Ask and answer, as in the example.

1.

they / oranges? → lemons

Q: Are they oranges?

A: No, they aren't. They are lemons.

2.

Jessica / a student? → a teacher

Q: _____

A: _____

3.

they / at the bus stop? → at the train station

Q: _____

A: _____

4.

you / in Korea last year? → in Egypt

Q: _____

A: _____

30 Unit 4

A Look at the example and practice with a partner. Use the words below or invent your own. (Repeat 3 times.)

1.

 Where is Lee Byunghun from? What is his job? How old is he?

 He is from Korea. He is an actor. He is 44 years old.

1.

Lee Byunghun / Korea
an actor / 44 years old

2.

Hugh Jackman / Australia
a movie star / 46 years old

3.

Kate Winslet / England
an actress / 39 years old

4.

Jackie Chan / Hong Kong
an action movie star / 60 years old

5.

 Were you at home yesterday?

 No, I wasn't. I was in class yesterday.

5.

at home? → No / in class

6.

at the park? → No / at the library

7.

in Paris? → No / in London

B Work with a partner. Ask and answer questions using the prompts below, as in the example.

1. you / at a party
2. Olivia / at the museum
3. Tom and Jane / at the movie theater
4. Cindy / at the beach
5. Anita / at home
6. you and your friends / at the shopping center
7. you / at a restaurant

Where were you at 7 o'clock yesterday?

I was at a party.

Your turn now.

A **Complete the sentences with the simple present or present progressive of the verbs in brackets.**

1. Mary usually _____walks_____ (walk) to school, but today she _____is riding_____ (ride) a bicycle to school.

2. They usually _____ (watch) TV, but today they _____ (have) a party.

3. I usually _____ (drink) tea, but today I _____ (drink) milk.

4. She _____ (visit) her grandmother now. She _____ (visit) her grandmother every week.

B **Fill in the blanks with the simple present or present progressive.**

William is a firefighter. He _____drives_____ (drive) a big red fire engine and he _____ (fight) fires. Now, he _____ (put) water onto the fire. He _____ (wear) a helmet.

C **Answer the questions below using the present progressive tense. Refer to the schedule below.**

This is Peter's schedule for next week:

MONDAY	Play tennis with my sister
TUESDAY	Meet Isabel
WEDNESDAY	Go to the movie theater with Bob
THURSDAY	Go to the doctor at 1:30
FRIDAY	Fly to New York

1. Q: What is Peter doing on Wednesday?

   A: He is going to the movie theater with Bob on Wednesday. _____

2. Q: What is Peter doing on Monday?

   A: _____

3. Q: What is Peter doing on Thursday?

   A: _____

4. Q: What is Peter doing on Friday?

   A: _____

5. What is Peter doing on Tuesday?

   A: _____

D Put these sentences into the past. Use the past forms of the verb *be*.

Today		Yesterday
1. I am at home.	→	I was at home yesterday.
2. Jane and Tom are tired.	→	_____
3. It's a sunny day.	→	_____
4. We aren't at work.	→	_____
5. You aren't at school.	→	_____

E Change each sentence into a *yes/no* question using the words in brackets.

1. Kevin's father drives fast. (your brother)

    → Does your brother drive fast? _____

2. Steve plays the guitar every day. (Peter)

    → _____

3. Sarah goes shopping on Mondays. (Ava and Cindy)

    → _____

4. Mother watches TV in the afternoon. (the children)

    → _____

F Look at the pictures. Write questions and answers as in the example.

1.

Q: Is she playing soccer? _____

A: No, she isn't. She is playing tennis. _____

she / play soccer?

2.

Q: _____

A: _____

he / drive to work?

3.

Q: _____

A: _____

they / watch TV?

Unit 5 Simple Past 1

- Read and answer the questions.
  1. Who is the artist?
  2. Where is the painting *Mona Lisa* now?
  3. Who are your favorite artists?
  4. What are your favorite paintings?

Unit Focus

▶ Affirmatives vs. Negatives
▶ *Yes/No* Questions
▶ *Used To*: Past Habits

Every day, 15,000 people visit the Louvre museum in Paris. Most of them want to see the *Mona Lisa*. Leonardo da Vinci started the painting in 1503 and he finished it about four years later. Leonardo was Italian, but in 1516, he moved to France with the painting. The King of France liked it and the *Mona Lisa* stayed in France.

Learn & Practice 1

Simple Past: Affirmatives vs. Negatives

- We use the simple past to talk about actions and situations that began and ended in the past.
- To form the simple past of regular verbs, we add *-ed* or *-d* to the base form of the verb.
- To make the negative of the simple past, we add *did not (= didn't)* before the base verb.

We **didn't visit** Rome.
We **visited** Athens.

Anna **didn't play** baseball yesterday.
She **played** soccer.

My mom **didn't wash** the car.
She **washed** the dishes.

Affirmative		**Negative**	
I/We/You He/She/It/They	**worked**.	I/We/You He/She/It/They	**did not** work. (= **didn't** work.)

A Complete the following sentences with the simple past of the verbs in brackets.

1. It ___rained___ (rain) yesterday.　　2. Bob _____ (not wait) for the bus.

3. First she _____ (open) the windows.　4. They _____ (not work) on Tuesday.

5. He _____ (stay) in the office.　　6. We _____ (not watch) TV last night.

Simple Past: *Yes/No* Questions

- To make a *yes/no* question, we put *did* at the beginning of the sentence. We always use the base verb after the subject.
- We often use *did* in short answers to questions.

Question		
Did Nancy **listen to** K-pop music yesterday?		
	Yes, she **did**.	**No**, she **didn't**. She **cleaned** her room.

Did	*Subject*	*Base Verb*	*Answers*	
Did	I/we/you he/she/it/they	dance?	Yes, I/we/he... **did**.	No, I/we/he... **didn't**.

Ⓐ Make *yes/no* questions and complete the short answers.

1. She practiced the piano. Q: *Did she practice the piano?* A: No, *she didn't* .

2. He enjoyed his vacation. Q: _____ A: Yes, _____ .

3. They liked the movie. Q: _____ A: No, _____ .

4. It rained all day. Q: _____ A: Yes, _____ .

5. I watched the discussion. Q: _____ A: No, _____ .

Ⓑ Make simple past questions using the words in brackets.

1. Peter enjoyed the food, but ____ *did he enjoy the music?* ____ (the music?)

2. Lisa listened to everything, but _____ (remember it?)

3. You liked the book, but _____ (the movie?)

4. You gave them some help, but _____ (any money?)

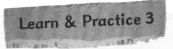
Used To: Past Habits

- *Used to do* is past. We use it to talk about past habits or things that do not happen anymore. It has the same form in all persons, singular and plural.
- We form questions and negations with the helping verb *did / did not* (= *didn't*), the subject, and the verb "*use*" without -*d*.

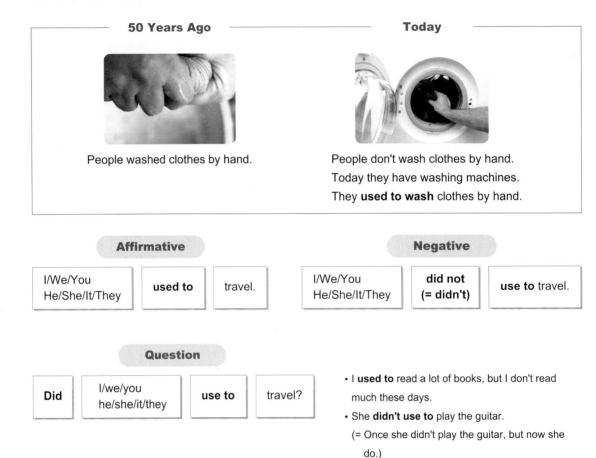

50 Years Ago ──────────── **Today**

People washed clothes by hand.

People don't wash clothes by hand.
Today they have washing machines.
They **used to wash** clothes by hand.

Affirmative

| I/We/You He/She/It/They | **used to** | travel. |

Negative

| I/We/You He/She/It/They | **did not** (= **didn't**) | **use to** travel. |

Question

| **Did** | I/we/you he/she/it/they | **use to** | travel? |

- I **used to** read a lot of books, but I don't read much these days.
- She **didn't use to** play the guitar.
  (= Once she didn't play the guitar, but now she do.)
- **Did** Tom **use to** live in the countryside?

Ⓐ Complete the sentences with the correct form of *used to* and the verbs in brackets.

1. I ___*didn't use to watch*___ (not / watch) the news, but now I watch it every day.

2. My uncle _____ (drink) a lot of coffee, but now he prefers to drink tea.

3. We _____ (live) in the countryside, but we live in the city now.

4. Kevin and I _____ (not / like) each other, but now we're good friends.

5. My sister _____ (play) the violin, but now she doesn't.

A Look at the pictures and prompts. Write questions and answers as in the example.

1.

Tom / play basketball / yesterday?
→ No / paint a picture

Q: Did Tom play basketball yesterday?

A: No, he didn't. He painted a picture.

2.

Olivia / go to the movie / last night?
→ No / listen to music

Q: _____

A: _____

3.

it / rain here / last month?
→ No / snow here

Q: _____

A: _____

4.

Sunny / watch a DVD / last night?
→ No / talk to John / on the phone

Q: _____

A: _____

_____

B Change this paragraph from the simple presnt to the simple past tense.

Jason is a student at the City College of San Francisco. He wants to be a science teacher, and he needs to take many science classes. He likes his classes. In his free time, he plays volleyball with his friends. His family is in Korea, and he sometimes visits them.

Five years ago, Jason _____

_____

_____

C Write four sentences about what you did yesterday.

1. Yesterday, I stayed at home and listened to music.

2. _____

3. _____

4. _____

5. _____

D Compare the way of life of the Inuit in the past with their way of life today. The Inuit used to be called "Eskimos". What did the Inuit use to do? Use the information and the phrases below.

traditional sled (qamutik)

Inuk in a kayak

Past: travel by dogsled
Past: get light from oil lamps
Past: travel by kayak
Past: live in igloos and tents
Past: hunt caribous with arrows

Now: travel by snowmobile
Now: have electric light bulbs
Now: travel by floatplane
Now: live in modern houses
Now: hunt caribous with rifles

1. The Inuit used to travel by dogsled. Now, they don't anymore. They travel by snowmobile.

2. _____

3. _____

4. _____

5. _____

E Look at the picture and say what people did and didn't do in those days. Write sentences in the affirmative or negative. Use the simple past tense.

1. Children / have / smartphones
   → Children didn't have smartphones.

2. People / watch / television
   → _____

3. A lot of women / stay / at home
   → _____

4. Children / eat / hamburgers
   → _____

5. Homes / have / computers
   → _____

6. Mothers / wash / clothes / by hand
   → _____

A Look at the example and practice with a partner. Use the words below or invent your own. (Repeat 3 times.)

I.

 Did Ava visit Spain last week?

 No, she didn't visit Spain. She visited Seoul.

1.  Ava / visit Spain / last week?
→ No / visit Seoul

2.  the girl / clean the house / last Saturday?
→ No / wash the car

3.  Joseph and Janet / watch a movie on television / yesterday?
→ No / visit their grandparents

4.  they / walk to the city center / yesterday?
→ No / stay at home

B Work with a partner. Take turns using *Did you use to...?*

 Did you use to bite your nails?

No, I didn't.

Your turn now!

Likes and dislikes
1. hate having baths and showers?
2. enjoy listening to fairy

Habits
1. bite your nails?
2. suck your thumb?
3. sleep with your parents?

When you were a little child...

Appearance
1. wear glasses?
2. have a different kind of hair style?
3. be fat/slim?

Hobbies and games
1. collect stamps or coins?
2. enjoy playing hide-and-seek?

Personality
1. be very shy?
2. be very naughty?
3. be very aggressive?
4. be happy?

• Read and answer the questions.
1. When was Cristiano Ronaldo born?
2. How was Ronaldo as a student?
3. What did he do in his free time?
4. Who is your favorite soccer player?

Cristiano Ronaldo was born on February 5, 1985 on the island of Madeira. He grew up in a small house in the city of Funchal. As s child, Ronaldo wasn't a good student. He spent all his free time playing soccer with his friends. He began playing soccer for a youth team in Madeira. He went to Manchester United in 2003. He became famous in England. He became a superstar around the world. Now, he is the most expensive player in soccer history.

Unit Focus

▶ Spelling Rules
▶ Irregular Verbs
▶ Time Clauses with *Before* and *After*

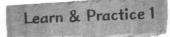
Learn & Practice 1

Spelling Rules of the Simple Past

- To form the affirmative past tense of most regular verbs:

smell → smell**ed** walk → walk**ed** help → help**ed** cross → cross**ed** visit → visit**ed** need → need**ed**	• Add **-ed** to most verbs.
arrive → arriv**ed** hope → hop**ed** invite → invit**ed** like → lik**ed**	• If a verb end in **-e**, add **-d**.
stud**y** → stud**ied** cr**y** → cr**ied** tr**y** → tr**ied** fl**y** → fl**ied**	• If a verb ends in a **consonant + -y**, change the **-y** to **-i** before the **-ed**.
sto**p** → stop**ped** pla**n** → plan**ned** prefe**r** → prefer**red**	• If a verb ends in a **vowel + a consonant**, **double the consonant** before the **-ed**.

Anna **graduated** last summer. I **wanted** to take her picture, so she **smiled** and I **photographed** her with her father.

Ⓐ Complete the sentences with the simple past of the verbs in brackets.

1. I ___decided___ (decide) to have a dinner party.
2. They _____ (invite) eight people.

3. A fire _____ (start) in the oven.
4. I _____ (brush) my teeth.

5. The baby _____ (cry) all day.
6. It _____ (stop) at lunchtime.

Simple Past: Irregular Verbs

- Some verbs do not have *-ed* forms. They each have different changes. Their past forms are irregular.

Base Form		Past Form
buy	→	bought
see	→	saw
go	→	went
make	→	made
give	→	gave
have	→	had
come	→	came
eat	→	ate

Base Form		Past Form
hear	→	heard
sit	→	sat
meet	→	met
speak	→	spoke
take	→	took
drink	→	drank
stand	→	stood
write	→	wrote

Base Form		Past Form
sleep	→	slept
teach	→	taught
ride	→	rode
leave	→	left
fly	→	flew
find	→	found
wear	→	wore
lose	→	lost

We **went** to a haunted house.
We **saw** a ghost there.

Q: When did Walter leave for Europe?
A: He **left** for Europe three days ago.

A Change the sentences to the past tense.

1.

Kathy drinks milk.
Kathy drank milk.

2.

Peter rides his bicycle.
_____

3.

I study for the chemistry test.
_____

4.

They make a model plane.
_____

5.

We eat lunch.
_____

6.

She goes to Africa.
_____

Simple Past: Time Clauses with *Before* and *After*

- *Before* and *after* tell us about time. A time clause begins with words such as *before* or *after*.
- A time clause has a subject and a verb, but it is not a complete sentence.
- A time clause must be connected to a main clause to form a complete sentence.
- A time clause can come in front of a main clause. A time clause can also follow a main clause. The meaning is the same, although it is more emphatic at the beginning.
- If the time clause comes first, it has a comma after it.

After we finished our homework, we took a walk.

I finished my homework **before I went to bed**.

Main Clause	Time Clause
I finished my homework We took a walk	**before I went to bed.** **after we finished our homework.**

Time Clause	Main Clause
Before I went to bed, **After we finished our homework,**	I finished my homework. we took a walk.

A Underline the time clauses in the sentences. Then rewrite the sentences by changing the order of the clauses.

1. After she ate dinner, she went to the movies.
   → *She went to the movies after she ate dinner.*

2. He had lunch before he finished his work.
   → _____

3. She got a good job after she graduated.
   → _____

4. After he did the dishes, he watched TV.
   → _____

A The sentences below are NOT true. First, make them negative. Then use Tom's calendar to write true sentences.

Tom's Week

Monday	Tuesday	Friday	Saturday	Sunday
go to the movies	clean my room	write an email to friends	sleep late	study and watch TV

1. Tom went to work on Monday.
   → Tom didn't go to work on Monday.
   → He went to the movies on Monday.

2. Tom did his laundry on Sunday.
   → _____
   → _____

3. Tom went out to dinner on Saturday.
   → _____
   → _____

4. Tom bought a pink wallet on Friday.
   → _____
   → _____

B Say which of these activities you did or didn't do yesterday.

play a sport	go to the library	speak English	go shopping
write an email	do my homework	watch television	meet friends
sleep late	buy some books	drink some orange juice	read some comic books

1. I didn't go shopping yesterday.
2. I read some comic books yesterday.
3. _____
4. _____
5. _____
6. _____
7. _____
8. _____
9. _____
10. _____

C Combine the two sentences about the pictures. Write one sentence with *after* and another with *before*.

1. He brushed his teeth. He went to bed.
   → After he brushed his teeth, he went to bed.
   → Before he went to bed, he brushed his teeth.

2. They got married. They had a baby.
   → _____
   → _____

3. She succeeded. She helped poor people.
   → _____
   → _____

4. He learned to walk. He rode a bicycle.
   → _____
   → _____

D Look at the pictures and prompts. Write questions and answers, as in the example.

1. Olivia / eat / a sandwich / last night?
   → No / eat / a hamburger

   Q: Did Olivia eat a sandwich last night?
   A: No, she didn't. She ate a hamburger.

2. Kathy / break / her ankle / two days ago?
   → No / hurt / her knee

   Q: _____
   A: _____

3. Cindy and Mark / watch / a DVD / yesterday?
   → No / go / to the movie theater

   Q: _____
   A: _____
   _____

4. the girls / walk / in the park / yesterday?
   → No / ride / their bicycles

   Q: _____
   A: _____
   _____

A Look at the example and practice with a partner. Use the words below or invent your own. (Repeat 3 times.)

I.

 Jessica went somewhere yesterday.

 Did she go to the zoo?

 No, she didn't go to the zoo.
She went to the movie theater.

1.
Jessica / go somewhere
yesterday / go to the zoo?
→ No / to the movie theather

2.
Terrance / meet somebody
yesterday / meet his boss?
→ No / one of his friends

3.
Isabel / buy something
yesterday / buy a dress
→ No / a T-shirt

4.
Nancy / bring something
yesterday / bring a cake
→ No / a puppy

5.
Brian / repair something
yesterday / repair the car?
→ No / the computer

6.
they / go somewhere
yesterday / go to the park?
→ No / to the museum

B Work with a partner. Combine the two sentences into one sentence by using time clauses. Say one sentence with *after* and another with *before*.

First	have breakfast	First	hear the doorbell
Then	go to school	Then	open the door
First	have a shower	First	lock the door
Then	have breakfast	Then	turn off the lights
First	get dressed	First	watch television
Then	have breakfast	Then	go to bed

After I had breakfast, I went to school.
I had breakfast before I went to school.

Now your turn!

• Read and answer the questions.

1. What did the girls do yesterday?
2. What were the girls doing at 6:20 yesterday?
3. What were you doing at 7:00 yesterday evening?

Unit Focus

▶ Affirmatives
▶ Negatives
▶ Yes/No Questions

Yesterday the girls played soccer. They began at 5:00 and finished at 7:00. So at 6:00 they were playing soccer. (They started to play before 7:00 and they were still playing at 6:00 yesterday.)

"Were the girls playing soccer at 6:30 yesterday?"

"Yes, they were."

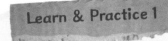

Learn & Practice 1

Past Progressive: Affirmatives

- We use the past progressive to talk about a past action at some point between its beginning and end.

Past	Now
Olivia **were sleeping** at this time yesterday. It was 10:00.	She **is listening** to music now. It is 10:00.

Subject	Be Verb	Verb + -ing	
I/He/She/It/Tom/Mary, etc.	was	exercising.	I **was doing** my homework at 3 o'clock. They **were fighting** in the park.
You/We/They The boys / Tom and Mary, etc.	were		Kevin **was sitting** in class. The children **were watching** TV.

A Rewrite the sentences in the past progressive.

1. Jane runs very fast.　　　　　　　→ *Jane was running very fast.*

2. My mom does the dishes.　　　　 →

3. He studied hard for the test.　　 →

4. Sunny and Jessica ride a roller coaster.　→

Past Progressive: Negatives

- To make the negative of the past progressive, we use *not* after *was/were*.

They **weren't fighting** in the park.
They were jogging.

Tiffany **wasn't talking** on the phone.
She was having lunch.

Subject	Be + Not	Verb + -ing
I/He/She/It Tom/Mary, etc.	was not (= wasn't)	
You/We/They The boys / Tom and Mary, etc.	were not (= weren't)	working.

Nancy **wasn't drawing** a picture.

He **wasn't reading** a newspaper.

They **weren't working** at 10:00 yesterday.

(A) Look at the pictures and complete the sentences with the verbs in brackets. Use the past progressive tense.

1.

   Kathy ___wasn't reading___ (not / read) a book.
   She ___was listening___ (listen) to music.

2.

   They _____ (not / prepare) dinner.
   They _____ (ride) their bicycles.

3.

   The students _____ (not / take) classes.
   They _____ (walk) to school.

4.

   She _____ (not / brush) her teeth.
   She _____ (wash) her face.

Past Progressive: *Yes/No* Questions

- To make a *yes/no* question, we put *was* or *were* before the subject.

Q: **Was** Bob **painting** the house last
   Sunday at noon?
A: **Yes**, he **was**.

Q: **Were** Peter and Lisa **working** at
   9 o'clock last night?
A: **No**, they **weren't**. They were
   having dinner at a restaurant.

- We often use short answers in speaking and informal writing. Don't use contractions in affirmative short answers.

Be Verb	Subject	Verb + *-ing*
Was	I/he/she/it Tom/Mary, etc.	
Were	you/we/they the boys Tom and Mary, etc.	**sleeping?**

Q: **Were** you **sleeping** at 11:00 last night?
A: **Yes**, I **was**.

Q: **Was** she **riding** her bicycle?
A: **No**, she **wasn't**. She was surfing the Internet.

Ⓐ Use the prompts to make *yes/no* questions in the past progressive. Then complete the short answers.

1. She / smile at you
   Q: *Was she smiling at you?*   A: Yes, *she was*   .

2. He / write a composition
   Q: _____   A: No, _____ .

3. It / rain last night
   Q: _____   A: Yes, _____ .

4. they / study Korean
   Q: _____   A: No, _____ .

5. Jane / talk with Tom
   Q: _____   A: Yes, _____ .

6. William / wash his car
   Q: _____   A: No, _____ .

7. the women / sit in a cafe
   Q: _____   A: Yes, _____ .

A What were the people doing yesterday evening? Look at the pictures and complete the sentences with the phrases from the box. Use the past progressive tense.

sit at her desk	wash the dishes
play the drums	have dinner
see a scary movie	talk on the phone

1. At 9:00 Kelly _____was sitting at her desk_____.

2. At 8:30 they_____.

3. At 7:50 Cindy_____.

4. At 8:00 they_____.

5. At 9:30 she _____.

6. At 7:30 the man _____.

B Answer the questions using the negative from of the past progressive. Then add a statement with the phrases in brackets.

1.
(watch TV)

Q: Was Sunny having dinner when I called?

A: _No, she wasn't having dinner. She was watching TV._

2.
(sleep on the bed)

Q: Were Harper and Lily reading books?

A: _____

3.
(work very hard)

Q: Was James listening to the news when Emma phoned him?

A: _____

4.
(take pictures)

Q: Were the girls jogging in the park?

A: _____

C Look at the pictures and prompts. Make questions and answer them. Use the past progressive tense.

1.

she / drive the car?
→ No / jog

Q: Was she driving the car?
A: No, she wasn't. She was jogging.

2.

the boy / swim in the pool?
→ No / fly his kite

Q: _____
A: _____

3.

Kathy / water the plants?
→ No / take the subway

Q: _____
A: _____

D A very valuable painting was stolen last night at around 7:30 p.m. from the museum. Sherlock Holmes is asking Peter about his activities yesterday. Write questions and answers using the phrases below the pictures.

1.

take a shower

Q: What were you doing at 7:00?
A: I was taking a shower.

2.

walk in the park

Q: _____
A: _____

3.

eat lunch in the restaurant

Q: _____
A: _____

4.

do the laundry

Q: _____
A: _____

A Look at the example and practice with a partner. Use the words below or invent your own. (Repeat 3 times.)

1.

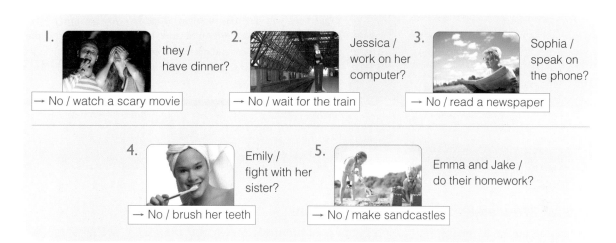

Were they having dinner?

No, they weren't.

What were they doing?

They were watching a scary movie.

1. they / have dinner?
→ No / watch a scary movie

2. Jessica / work on her computer?
→ No / wait for the train

3. Sophia / speak on the phone?
→ No / read a newspaper

4. Emily / fight with her sister?
→ No / brush her teeth

5. Emma and Jake / do their homework?
→ No / make sandcastles

B Work with a partner. Look at the pictures. Use the past progressive to describe the activities that were in progress.

What was Lisa doing at seven o'clock yesterday evening?

She was working out in the gym.

Your turn now!

Lisa / work out in the gym

Nick / make a phone call

your friends / chat with each other

Aiden and Lisa / wash the car

Jane / cook dinner

Susan / write a letter

Ava / read a novel

Unit 8 Past Progressive 2

- Read and answer the questions.
1. What were you doing at seven o'clock yesterday morning?
2. Have you ever seen a UFO in the sky?
3. Do you believe in aliens on other planets?

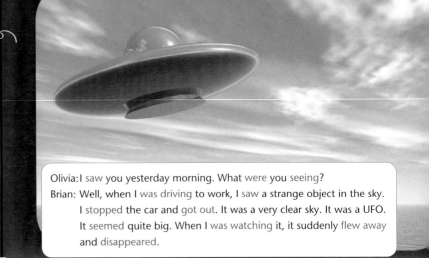

Unit Focus

▶ Information Questions
▶ Past Progressive and Simple Past

Olivia: I saw you yesterday morning. What were you seeing?
Brian: Well, when I was driving to work, I saw a strange object in the sky. I stopped the car and got out. It was a very clear sky. It was a UFO. It seemed quite big. When I was watching it, it suddenly flew away and disappeared.

Learn & Practice 1

Past Progressive: Information Questions

- To make an information question in the past progressive, we put *what, who, when, where, why,* or *how* before the verb *be*.

Q: **What was** Lisa **doing** an hour ago?
A: She was playing badminton.

Q: **Who was playing** the piano?
A: Linda was (playing the piano).

WH- Word	Be Verb	Subject	Verb + -ing
What When Where Why How Who*	was	I/he/she/it Tom/Mary, etc.	saying? going? working? running? watching?
	were	you/we/they the girls Tom and Mary, etc.	

*In formal written English, when *who* is an object or is part of a prepositional complement, it should be written as *whom*.

E.g. Whom (= Who) was she talking to?

- When *who* is the subject of a verb, we don't need a subject. In *Who was teaching you English?* the subject is *who*.

A Complete the questions. Use *was/were -ing*.

1. Q: <u>*Where were you living*</u> (you, live, where) in 1999? A: In Korea.

2. Q: _____ (Sunny, drive, why) so fast? A: Because she was late.

3. Q: _____ (they, go, where) at 8:00? A: To the hospital.

4. Q: _____ (Jane, do, what)? A: She was running to the bus stop.

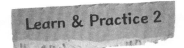

Past Progressive and Simple Past

- We use the past progressive to describe an action in progress at a particular time in the past.

- We use the simple past to talk about actions and situations that began and ended in the past.

Past Progressive	**Simple Past**

Steve and Nancy **were watching** TV at 7 o'clock yesterday evening.

Jessica **went** to India in 1998.

- We use the past progressive to talk about actions that were in progress and interrupted by another action in the past.

While Alice **was driving** to the bank, the cell phone **rang**.

Alice **was driving** to the bank. (longer action)
The cell phone **rang**. (shorter action)

I **was watching** TV when someone **knocked** at the door.

I **was watching** TV. (longer action)
Someone **knocked** at the door. (shorter action)

A Complete the sentences. Use the past progressive of the verbs in brackets.

1. When I _____was driving_____ (drive) down the hill, I saw a strange woman.

2. While Alice _____ (run), something hit her and she fell down.

3. Isabella _____ (watch) TV when her mother came in.

4. When the light went out, Jessica _____ (study) Korean.

5. _____ you _____ (drive) your car when the accident happened?

6. It began to rain while Tom and I _____ (walk) to school this morning.

B Complete the answers with the past progressive of the verbs in brackets.

1. Q: What were you doing when I called last night?
   A: I _____was having_____ (have) dinner with my family.

2. Q: Where were you going when I saw you yesterday?
   A: I _____ (go) to the library with my friend.

3. Q: What was your mother doing when she burned her hand?
   A: She _____ (iron) her shirts.

4. Q: What were your friends doing when you arrived at the party?
   A: They _____ (sing and dance) together.

C Complete the sentences. Use the simple past or the past progressive of the verbs in brackets.

1. I _____was studying_____ (study) in the library when I ___saw___ (see) her.

2. While I _____ (wash) the dishes last night, I _____ (get) a phone call from my best friend.

3. My friend Tiffany _____ (come) while I _____ (eat) dinner last night.

4. My mom _____ (brush) her teeth when I _____ (arrive) at home.

5. Tom _____ (sleep) when the cell phone _____ (ring).

6. Kelly _____ (wait) for a bus when it _____ (begin) to rain.

A Last Saturday Mr. and Mrs. Smith invited some of their children's friends to spend the afternoon at their house. Look at the picture and answer the questions.

1. Paul / play   2. Ted / wash   3. Cynthia / watch   4. Mrs. Smith / eat
7. Mr. Smith / clean
6. boy / girl / study
5. boys / read
8. girls / drink   9. children / play   10. girl / paint

1. Q: Was Paul eating a hamburger?   A: No, he wasn't eating a hamburger.
   Q: What was he doing?   A: He was playing volleyball.

2. Q: Was Ted surfing the net?   A: _____
   Q: What was he doing?   A: _____

3. Q: Was Cynthia washing the dishes?   A: _____
   Q: What was she doing?   A: _____

4. Q: Was Mrs. Smith cleaning the house?   A: _____
   Q: What was she doing?   A: _____

5. Q: What were the boys doing?   A: _____

6. What were the boy and the girl doing?   A: _____

7. Q: Was Mr. Smith speaking on the phone?   A: _____
   Q: What was he doing?   A: _____

8. What were the girls doing?   A: _____

9. Were the children playing basketball?   A: _____

10. What was the girl painting?   A: _____

B Look at the pictures. Make sentences with the prompts. Use the simple past or the past progressive and *while* or *when*, as in the example.

1. Jeff / eat / a hamburger / the email / arrive (when)
   → *Jeff was eating a hamburger when the email arrived.*

2. Kathy / drive / to the bank / the cell phone / ring (While)
   → _____

3. William / run / in the street / it / start / raining (when)
   → _____

4. Bill / watch / a scary movie / his friend / arrive (when)
   → _____

C Look at the pictures and cues below. Write questions using the prompts in brackets and answer them.

1. (when / you / call / her / yesterday)
   Q: *What was Sarah doing when you called her yesterday?*
   A: *She was swimming when I called her yesterday.*

   Sarah: swim

2. (when / you / come home / yesterday)
   Q: _____
   A: _____

   Ava: read a novel

3. (when / you / come home / from school)
   Q: _____
   A: _____

   your mother: do the laundry

A Look at the example and practice with a partner. Use the words below or invent your own. (Then change roles and practice again.)

1.

 What was Jane doing when the earthquake hit?

 She was eating soup.

 What did she do when it happened?

 She stayed under the table.

1.

Jane / eat soup / stay under the table

2.

Linda / talk on the phone / stand up

3.

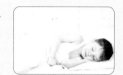

Peter / sleep / protect his head with a pillow

4.

Rachel / sit on the bench / start to cry

5.

they / watch a movie / stay away from windows

6.

Karen / have breakfast / go outside

B Work with a partner. Look at the pictures. What do you think the person was doing in each situation?

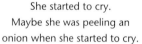
She started to cry. Maybe she was peeling an onion when she started to cry.

she / start to cry (result)
→ peel an onion

he / fall down (result)
→ go down the stairs

Your turn now!

he / fall asleep (result)
→ watch TV

she / laugh loudly (result)
→ speak on the phone

he / hurt his finger (result)
→ cook

A **Complete the sentences. Use the simple past or the past progresive of the verbs in brackets.**

1. It ___began___ (begin) to rain while she ___was riding___ (ride) her bicycle.

2. My father _____ (drive) when he _____ (crash) into a tree.

3. My sister _____ (watch) TV when the doorbell _____ (ring).

4. The teacher _____ (correct) the homework while we _____ (work) in the classroom.

B **Look at the pictures and write what these people used to do in their childhood.**

1.

Lisa / tennis

Lisa used to play tennis in her childhood.

2.

Kevin / a lot of pizza

_____

C **Look at the pictures and prompts. Write sentences using the simple past or the past progressive and *while* or *when*, as in the example.**

1.

Nancy / sleep / the cell phone / ring (when)

→ Nancy was sleeping when the cell phone rang.

2.

Alice / drive / a man / cross / the street (While)

→ _____

3.

they / walk / in the park / it / start / raining (when)

→ _____

4.

my dad / brush his teeth / I / arrive at home (when)

→ _____

D Use the prompts to write simple past tense sentences.

1. yesterday / I / be / tired / during the day   _Yesterday I was tired during the day._

2. you / be / sick / last week   _____

3. you / have / a cough and a fever   _____

4. she / have / a bad headache   _____

5. this morning / Kevin / be / nervous   _____

E Complete the following sentences with the simple past of the verbs in brackets.

1. I ___broke___ (break) my arm last week.

2. My brother _____ (drive) to the hospital.

3. You _____ (wake) up at 7:00.

4. She _____ (go) to the doctor at noon.

5. They _____ (come) to visit you.

6. He _____ (eat) a healthy breakfast.

7. Teresa _____ (do) some exercises.

8. She _____ (take) some vitamins.

F Combine the two sentences. Write one sentence with *before* and another with *after*.

1. We arrived at the airport. The plane landed.
   - → _Before we arrived at the airport, the plane landed._
   - → _After the plane landed, we arrived at the airport._

2. I went to a movie. I finished my homework.
   - → _____
   - → _____

3. They watched TV. They got home from school.
   - → _____
   - → _____

G Look at the pictures. Ask and answer questions using the prompts suggested.

1.	2.	3.
she / wait for a train	Dad / wash the dishes	they / have lunch

1. Q: _What was she doing?_
   A: _She was waiting for a train._

2. Q: _____
   A: _____

3. Q: _____
   A: _____

Unit 9 The Future Tense 1

- Read and answer the questions.
1. Will people go on vacation to the moon?
2. Will people find life on other planets?
3. What are you going to do this weekend?
4. What are you going to do this summer?

Unit Focus
- ▶ Future: *Be Going To*
- ▶ Future: *Will*
- ▶ *Be Going To* vs. *Will*

> I am going to go to the beach tomorrow. I will spend the whole day there. I will call James and ask him to come with me. He will say yes, I hope. We will have a great time!

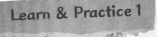
Learn & Practice 1

Future: *Be Going To*

- We use *be going to* + base verb to talk about our plans that we have already decided to do.
- We also use *be going to* for a prediction based on the present situation when we think something is going to happen very soon.

Future Prediction

The ladder is moving.
Tom **is going to** fall.

Planned Action

They **are going to** get married on Saturday.

- To make negative forms, we put *not* after the verb be.
- In a *yes/no* question, put *am*, *is*, or *are* before the subject.

Subject + *Be*	*Not Going To*	Base Verb
I am		
He/She/It is	**not** going to	eat.
You/We/They are		

I'm **not** going to watch TV tonight.
Sarah **isn't** going to sell her car.
We **aren't** going to travel to Singapore.

Be + Subject	*Going To*	Base Verb
Am I		
Is he/she/it	**going to**	go?
Are you/we/they		

Q: **Are** you **going to** watch a movie?
A: **Yes**, I **am**. / **No**, I'm **not**.
Q. **What is** she **going to** do tonight?
A: She**'s going to** read novels.

A Complete the sentences with *be going to* and the verbs in brackets. Then change them into questions and check.

		Future Prediction	Prior Plan

1. Kevin ____is going to paint____ (paint) the house tomorrow.
   → Is Kevin going to paint the house tomorrow?

   Future Prediction: ☐ Prior Plan: ☑

2. Look at the sky! It _____ (rain).
   → Look at the sky! _____

   Future Prediction: ☐ Prior Plan: ☐

3. You _____ (watch) TV tonight.
   → _____

   Future Prediction: ☐ Prior Plan: ☐

4. They _____ (buy) a new car next month.
   → _____

   Future Prediction: ☐ Prior Plan: ☐

Learn & Practice 2

Future: *Will*

- We use *will* + base verb for the future to make predictions about what we think will happen.
- We also use *will* + base verb for the future when we decide to do something at the time of speaking.

Future Prediction

I **will** be an astronaut.

Decision at the Time of Speaking

Q: **Will** you walk with me?
A: **Yes**, I **will**.

Subject	Will Not	Base Verb	
I He/She/It We/You/They	will not (= won't)	go.	It **won't** rain tomorrow. They **won't** get on a bus. Tiffany **won't** ride her bicycle.

Will	Suject	Base Verb	
Will	I he/she/it we/you/they	go?	Q: **Will** you call me later tomorrow? A: **Yes**, I **will**. Q: **Will** she leave for Chicago next week? A: **No**, she **won't**.

A Make negative sentences. Then make *yes/no* questions and complete the short answers.

1. He will go to the library. → He won't go to the library. _____

   → Q: Will he go to the library? _____ A: No, __he won't__ .

2. They will eat oranges. → _____

   → Q: _____ A: Yes, _____ .

3. She will buy new clothes. → _____

   → Q: _____ A: No, _____ .

4. It will rain tomorrow. → _____

   → Q: _____ A: Yes, _____ .

Learn & Practice 3

Be Going To vs. *Will*

- We don't use *will* for the future when plans were made before this moment.
- We don't use *be going to* for the future when we decide to do something at the time of speaking.

A: What are your plans for tomorrow?
B: We**'re going to** see a scary movie.
NOT: We **will** see a scary movie. (X)

These shoes are very comfortable.
I **will** buy them.
NOT: I'm **going to** buy them. (X)

A Complete the sentences using *will* or *be going to*.

1.

   They __are going to get__ (get) married next month.

2.

   It's very hot here. I_____ (open) the window.

3.

   A: I'm very thirsty.
   B: I _____ (bring) you a glass of water.

4.

   My friends and I _____ (go) to the movie theater tomorrow.

A What's going to happen? Look at the pictures and prompts and complete the speech bubbles. Use the future *be going to*.

Where's Olivia? _She's going_
to miss the plane.

1.

she / miss / the plane

I am in the supermarket.
_____

2.

I / buy / some fruit

Oh, no! _____
_____

3.

Kevin / fall into the river

Look! _____

4.

it / rain

B Read the statements, then make questions and complete the short answers.

1. Q: _Will you be at the library tomorrow night?_____

   A: Yes, _____I will_____. (I'll be at the library tomorrow night.)

2. Q: _____

   A: Yes, _____. (People will live in space colonies.)

3. Q: _____

   A: No, _____. (The train won't be on time.)

4. Q: _____

   A: No, _____. (Hunter and Sunny won't be at the party.)

5. Q: _____

   A: Yes, _____. (Ava will arrive in Hong Kong next week.)

6. Q: _____

   A: Yes, _____. (We'll travel around the world in an hour by space shuttle.)

C Sophia is a very busy businesswoman. Look at her calendar and write sentences with the future *be going to*, as in the example.

Monday:
Have lunch with John (O)
Go to the movie theater (X)

Tuesday:
Attend a meeting from 8:00 to 10:00 (O)
Have brunch with Tom (X)

Wednesday:
Go to a computer conference on 58th street (O)
Take a yoga class (X)

Thursday:
Give a presentation to boss at 12:00 (O)

Friday:
Take the train to Boston (O)

Saturday:
Meet Lisa outside the movie theater at 7:00 (O)
Eat dinner in a restaurant (X)

1. On Monday, she's going to have lunch with John.
   She isn't going to go to the movie theater.

2. _____

3. _____

4. _____

5. _____

6. _____

D Look at the pictures. Use the prompts to make questions and answers as in the example. Use the future *be going to*.

1. Linda / take the dog for a walk / tomorrow?
   → No / go shopping

   Q: Is Linda going to take the dog for a walk tomorrow?
   A: No, she isn't. She's going to go shopping.

2. Aiden / take a bus to work / tomorrow morning?
   → No / ride his bicycle to work

   Q: _____
   A: _____

3. the children / watch a DVD / next Wednesday?
   → No / study math

   Q: _____
   A: _____

A Look at the example and practice with a partner. Use the words below or invent your own. (Then change roles and practice again.)

1.

1. clean my room   study chemisty

I'm going to clean my room this weekend. What are you going to do this weekend?

I'm going to study chemistry.

2.
go fishing   visit Seoul

3. take swimming lessons   go sports camp

4.
spend time with my friends   go to the beach

5. see a movie   visit my grandparents

B Which of the following events do you think will happen in the future? Check your answers and then discuss.

	Agree	Disagree
1. We'll have fewer household chores because robots will do the work.		
2. Aliens will invade the earth.		
3. Global warming will wipe out many animal species.		
4. People will live for 150 years or more.		
5. There will be no more schools because children will learn at home through the Internet.		
6. Flying cars will solve the problem of traffic jams.		
7. Will there be a cure for cancer in 20 years?		

The Future Tense 2

• Read and answer the questions.

1. Is Jacob going to play tennis next Tuesday?
2. What are you going to do this weekend?
3. What will you do if there is no class tomorrow?

Unit Focus

▶ *Be Going To*, Present Progressive, Simple Present
▶ Future Time Clauses
▶ Future Conditional Sentences

Lucy: What are you doing next Tuesday?
Jacob: I'm going to do an experiment. I read something interesting in a science book yesterday. If you keep a goldfish in a dark room for days, it will eventually turn white! Isn't it amazing?

Learn & Practice 1

Future: *Be Going To*, Present Progressive, Simple Present

- We use *be going to* for plans and intentions for the (near) future. We use *be going to* when there is evidence that something is going to happen in the near future.
- The simple present is used for events that are part of a timetable or schedule. While the events are in the future, their existence is already established in the present, so we use the simple present.
- We use the present progressive to talk about future plans. We often use verbs like *go, come, see, meet, stay, have,* and *leave.* The present progressive for the future and *be going to* have similar meanings.

He **is having** a meeting with his boss in an hour. (He has already arranged it.)

Tom **is going to fall off** the chair. (It is certain. There is visible evidence.)

My plane **leaves** at 9:00 tonight. (We're talking about a timetable.)

Ⓐ Complete the sentences with *be going to*, the simple present, or the present progressive.

1. Susan ___is flying___ (fly) to New York in two hours.

2. It _____ (rain). There are dark clouds in the sky.

3. The concert _____ (begin) at eight tonight.

Future Time Clauses with *When, Before,* and *After*

- A future time clause can begin with *when*, *before*, and *after*.
- When a time clause refers to the future, we use the simple present. We don't use *will* or *be going to* in a future time clause.
- We can put the time clause before or after the main clause. They both have the same meaning. Use a comma (,) after the time clause when it comes at the beginning.

After they **finish** their homework, they **will take** a walk.

When they **go** to Singapore next week, They**'re going to stay** at the Hilton Hotel.

Time Clasuse
After they finish their homework,

Main Clause
they will take a walk.

Main Clause
They're going to stay at the Hilton Hotel

Time Clause
when they go to Singapore next week.

A Use the given verbs to complete the sentences. Give a future meaning to the sentences.

1. go / get
   → Before I _____*get*_____ on the plane, I ___*will go*___ to the duty-free shop.

2. give / say
   → Before I _____ goodbye, I _____ you my address.

3. ask / call
   → When I _____ Bob tomorrow, I _____ him to come to my party.

4. go / finish
   → After he _____ his homework, he _____ to bed.

5. wear / go
   → When she _____ to the interview, she _____ her new suit.

Future Conditional Sentences

- We use future conditional sentences to describe what might happen in the future. One action depends on another one.
- The condition is what must happen first. It begins with the word *if*. We call this type of dependent clause an *if*-clause.
- In future conditional sentences, we use the simple present in an *if*-clause to express future time. We use a future tense in the main clause.
- We can put an *if*-clause before or after the main clause. They both have the same meaning. Use a comma (,) after the *if*-clause when it comes at the beginning.

If the weather **is** nice tomorrow, we**'ll go** fishing.   **I'm going to stay** home **if** it **rains** tomorrow.

If-Clause (Present)	Main Clause (Future)
If the weather is nice tomorrow,	we will go fishing.

Main Clause (Future)	*If*-Clause (Present)
I'm going to stay home	**if** it rains tomorrow.

Ⓐ Complete the sentences with the verbs in brackets. Use the simple present or *will*.

1.

If you ____go____ (go) to Paris, you will see the Eiffel Tower.

2.

If it's very hot, we _____ (go) to the beach.

3.

If you eat an apple a day, you _____ (be) healthy.

4.

If you _____ (throw) litter in the sea, you will pollute water.

A Look at Kevin's schedule and correct the sentences. Use the simple progressive.

1. He's watching a movie on Sunday morning.

   No, he's playing volleyball on Sunday morning.

2. He's staying at home on Monday afternoon.

   _____

3. He's having dinner with Lisa on Tuesday evening.

   _____

4. He's flying to Rome on Thursday night.

   _____

5. He's coming to the party on Friday afternoon.

   _____

6. He's playing tennis with Meg on Saturday morning.

   _____

Sunday
play volleyball / morning

Monday
see John Parker / afternoon

Tuesday
clean his bedroom / evening

Thursday
go to the theater / night

Friday
visit Madame Tussauds museum / afternoon

Saturday
leave for Mexico / morning

B Look at the pictures and make conditional sentences.

1.

Shawn must run very fast and he will win the race.

→ *If Shawn runs very fast, he will win the race. /*

   If Shawn doesn't run very fast, he won't win

   the race.

2.

Take the subway or you'll be late for work.

→ _____

   _____

   _____

3.

The purse will be expensive, so Olivia won't buy it.

→ _____

   _____

   _____

4.

Don't write on the desk! You'll be in trouble.

→ _____

   _____

   _____

C Combine the two sentences as in the example.

1. I will buy a new coat. I will go shopping tomorrow. (when)
   → When I go shopping tomorrow, I will buy a new coat.

2. Isabella will finish her homework this evening. She will take a walk. (after)
   → _____

3. Karen will do her homework. she's going to go home later in the evening. (after)
   → _____

4. I'm going to buy a scarf at the store. I will go home. (before)
   → _____

5. I will see William tomorrow. I will ask him to join us for dinner this weekend. (when)
   → _____

D Tiffany is going on a school trip tomorrow. Her mother is worried about her. Make sentences as in the example.

1. go out without a jacket at night / get a cold
   → If you go out without a jacket at night, you'll get a cold.

2. don't eat breakfast / be hungry
   → _____

3. eat too many chocolates / get fat
   → _____

4. go to bed early / not be tired the next day
   → _____

5. lie in the sun / get sunburned
   → _____

A Look at the example and practice with a partner. Use the words below or invent your own. (Then change roles and practice again.)

1.

the movie / start tomorrow?
→ at 11:30 tomorrow morning

1.
 What time does the movie start tomorrow?

 It starts at 11:30 tomorrow morning.

2.

Alex's plane / arrive tomorrow?
→ at 10:40 tomorrow morning

3.

the first train / leave tomorrow?
→ at 6:30 tomorrow morning

4.

the soccer game / begin tomorrow?
→ at 2:30 tomorrow afternoon

5.

go to an ice hockey match

5.
 What are your plans for this evening?

 I'm going to an ice hockey match.

6.

work with Christina

7.

have dinner with my family

8.

go to the Korean conversation club

B Interview!
Work with a partner. Ask questions and answer them as in the example.

What will you do if the weather is nice this weekend?
If the weather is nice this weekend, I'll go to the beach.
Your turn now!

1. What will you do if the weather is nice this weekend? _____

2. What will you do if class is canceled tomorrow? _____

3. What will you do if you don't study tonight? _____

4. What will you do if someone steals your smartphone? _____

Nouns and Articles

- Read and answer the questions.
1. Do you like comedies or action movies?
2. What kinds of movies do you like?
3. Is Harry Potter a wizard?

Unit Focus

▶ Nouns and Regular Nouns
▶ Count and Noncount Nouns
▶ Articles: *A/An* and *The*

Most **children** love the Harry Potter **books**. They are about **magic**. A **boy** and his **friends** fight many **enemies** and solve **mysteries**. They're **movies**, too. I like them.

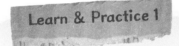

Nouns and Regular Nouns

- Common nouns are words for people, animals, places, or things. Most nouns are common nouns.
- Proper nouns are the names of specific people, places, or things. They always begin with a capital letter.

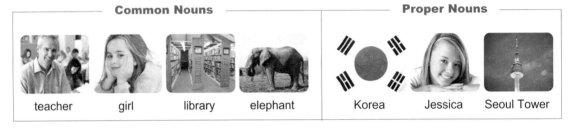

Common Nouns				**Proper Nouns**		
teacher	girl	library	elephant	Korea	Jessica	Seoul Tower

- We add *-s*, *-es*, *-ies*, or *-ves* to make the plurals of regular nouns.

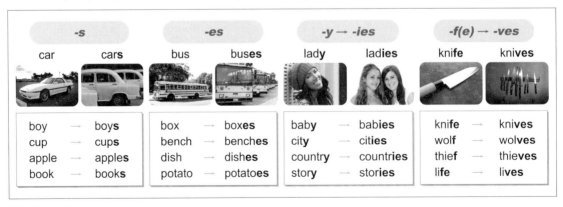

-s		**-es**		**-y → -ies**		**-f(e) → -ves**	
car	cars	bus	buses	lady	ladies	knife	knives
boy → boys		box → boxes		baby → babies		knife → knives	
cup → cups		bench → benches		city → cities		wolf → wolves	
apple → apples		dish → dishes		country → countries		thief → thieves	
book → books		potato → potatoes		story → stories		life → lives	

Irregular Plurals

Singular:	a man	a woman	a child	a foot	a mouse	a sheep	a fish
Plural:	**men**	**women**	**children**	**feet**	**mice**	**sheep**	**fish**

A Write the plural of the following words.

1. dish → _dishes_   2. country → _____   3. potato → _____

4. tomato → _____   5. box → _____   6. thief → _____

7. foot → _____   8. fish → _____   9. woman → _____

10. story → _____   11. bench → _____   12. leaf → _____

Learn & Practice 2

Count (= Countable) and Noncount (= uncountable) Nouns

- Count nouns can be in the singular or the plural. We put *a* before the noun in the singular when it begins with a consonant sound(*b, d, p,* etc.) and *an* when it begins with a vowel sound (*a, e, i, o, u*).
- Noncount nouns don't have plural forms. *A* and *an* are not used with noncount nouns.

| **an** orange | three orange**s** | rice (O)   **a** rice (X)   rice**s** (X) |

Noncount Nouns

a/an

Food: butter, salt, cheese, pepper, meat, bread, chocolate, honey, sugar
Liquids: coffee, water, tea, milk, wine, oil
Materials: gold, iron, silver, wood, paper, furniture, clothing
Abstract Nouns: beauty, love, happiness, experience
Others: hair, money, news, snow, weather, advice

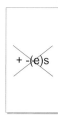
+ -(e)s

- These things are always plural in English.

shoes (sneakers)   pants   gloves

glass**es**   chopstick**s**   scissor**s**

Do you wear **glasses**?

Where are the **chopsticks**? I need them.

A Write C for count nouns and N for noncount nouns.

1. __N__ money   2. _____ teacher   3. _____ furniture   4. _____ monkey

5. _____ food   6. _____ soap   7. _____ house   8. _____ chair

9. _____ flower   10. _____ gold   11. _____ advice   12. _____ tooth

B Complete the sentences with the singular or plural form of the nouns in brackets.

1. There is a __book__ (book) on the table.

2. There are five _____ (pencil) on my desk.

3. There are two _____ (sheep) in the filed.

4. There is some _____ (cheese) in the fridge

5. How much _____ (water) is there on Earth?

6. There are two _____ (puppy) in the park.

Learn & Practice 3

Articles: *A/An* and *The*

- We can use *a/an* in front of singular count nouns. Remember that *a* and *an* mean one.
- We put *a* before a consonant and *an* before a vowel.
- We use *the* to talk about something specific or one and only. We use *the* with singular count nouns, plural count nouns, and noncount nouns to talk about something that has already been mentioned or is known.

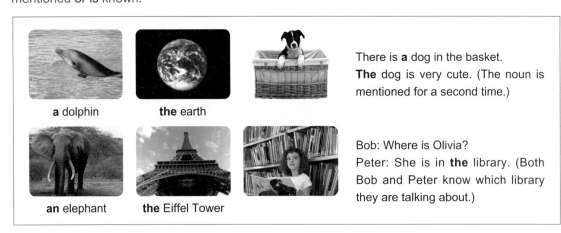

a dolphin   **the** earth

There is **a** dog in the basket. **The** dog is very cute. (The noun is mentioned for a second time.)

an elephant   **the** Eiffel Tower

Bob: Where is Olivia?
Peter: She is in **the** library. (Both Bob and Peter know which library they are talking about.)

A Complete the sentences using *a*, *an*, or *the*.

1. I live in __an__ apartment in the city. __The__ apartment is in __a__ big building.

2. I bought _____ book and _____ pen, but I lost _____ pen on my way home.

A Rewrite the sentences, adding *a*, *an*, or *the* where necessary.

1. Moon moves slowly round earth.

   → The moon moves slowly round the earth.

2. Sun is very hot today.

   → _____

3. I have two girls. Girls are at school.

   → _____

4. I don't have car or apartment.

   → _____

5. Prince of Wales is visiting our town next week.

   → _____

6. You can have apple or oranges. Apple is nice and sweet.

   → _____

B Look at the pictures. Read the questions and answer them as in the example.

1.
   Q: Are there balloons in the girl's hand?

   A: Yes, there are five balloons. _____

2.
   Q: Are there schoolbags in this picture?

   A: _____

3.
   Q: Are there women under the tree?

   A: _____

4.
   Q: Are there boxes in the man's hand?

   A: _____

C Fill in each blank with the plural form of the noun in brackets.

1. London, Paris, and Rome are ____cities____ (city).

2. The _____ (goose) chased the stranger down the path.

3. The _____ (leaf) are falling from the tree.

4. The _____ (watch) in this shop are expensive.

5. This room is for _____ (lady) only.

6. The cow was attacked by a pack of _____ (wolf).

7. The _____ (child) are playing in the garden.

D Look at the pictures and use the prompts to complete the sentences. Add *a*, *an*, or *the* where necessary.

the Pyramids	Jessica	Cindy	Dave

1. The Pyramids are _____ in Egypt _____.
   (Egypt / in)

2. Jessica practices _____.
   (piano / every day)

3. Cindy should take _____.
   (umbrella / this afternoon)

4. Dave has a puppy. _____.
   (puppy / really cute / is)

A Look at the example and practice with a partner. Use the words below or invent your own. (Then change roles and practice again.)

1.

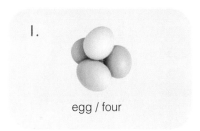

egg / four

1.

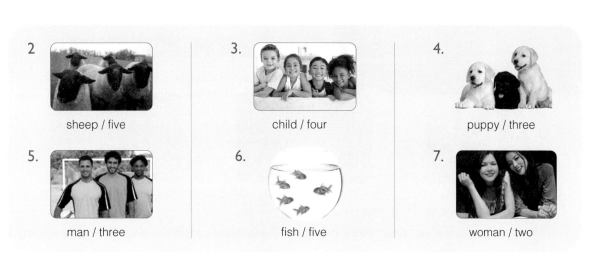

How many eggs are there in this picture?

There are four eggs.

2

sheep / five

3.

child / four

4.

puppy / three

5.

man / three

6.

fish / five

7.

woman / two

B Work with a partner. You are showing photographs from your holiday round the world to your partner. Look at the pictures and ask questions like *What's this?* or *What are these?* Then answer them, adding *a*, *an*, or *the* where necessary, as in the exampe.

1.

Colosseum

2.

Seoul Tower

What's this?

It's the Colosseum.

3.

gondolas

4.

Statue of Liberty

5.

palm trees

6.

windmill

Quantity Words

• Read and answer the questions.

1. Where is Alice?
2. Do they have any coffee?
3. How many slices of pizza can you eat?
4. How many different vegetables have you eaten today?

Unit *Focus*

▶ Units of Measure with Nouns
▶ *Some* and *Any*
▶ *Every*
▶ *Many, Much, A Lot Of*

Alice: Hello, Brian. I'm at the supermarket. What do I need to buy?
Brian: Hi, Alice! We don't need any coffee, but we need two cartons of milk.
Alice: Do we need any tea?
Brian: Oh, I have to check... Yes, you have to buy some tea.
Alice: Is that everything Brian?
Brian: Yes, that's everything. Bye-bye.
Alice: OK, bye-bye. See you at home.

Learn & Practice 1

Units of Measure wth Nouns

- We can count noncount nouns by using units of measure in front of them. They always have a prepositional phrase with *of*. For example, we can't count 'milk'. We can count 'bottles of milk', but we can't count 'milk' itself.

The waitress gave us **two glasses of** water with **three cups of** coffee.

a cup/glass of	water, milk, tea, juice, coffee
a slice/piece of	bread, pizza, toast, meat, cheese
a piece/sheet of	paper
a loaf of	bread, meat
a bottle of	milk, juice, wine, ink, shampoo
a tube of	toothpaste
a carton of	milk, juice

E.g. two glass**es** of juice, three slice**s** of pizza, four bottle**s** of milk

Ⓐ Look at the pictures. Choose and write as in the example.

coffee   bread   cheese   paper

1.   _a sheet/piece of paper_

2.   _____

Some and Any

- We use *some/any* to say the amount when we don't know exactly how many or how much.
- We use *some/any* for both count and noncount nouns.
- We use *some* in affirmative sentences with plural count nouns and with noncount singular nouns.
- We use *any* in negative sentences and in most questions.

I like this road. I can get **some** peace and quiet here.
There aren't **any** cars. There isn't **any** pollution.
There isn't **any** noise.

A Write *a(n)*, *some*, or *any*.

1. There is __an__ apple, and there is __some__ water.

2. There aren't _____ classes on Saturday.

3. I bought _____ cheese, but I didn't buy _____ bread.

4. Is there _____ bank near here?

Every

- We use *every* with singular count nouns. If *every* + noun is the subject, the verb is always singular.
- *Every* plus a singular noun means the same thing as *all the* with a plural noun.

Every woman **is** smiling. = **All the** women **are** smiling.
Every woman **is** an athlete. = **All the** women **are** athletes.
Every woman **has** a medal. = **All the** women **have** a medal.

A Complete the sentences with *every* or *all*.

1. __Every__ student wears a uniform.

2. _____ the rooms have a balcony.

3. _____ worker starts at 8 a.m.

4. _____ the students passed the exam.

Many, Much, A Lot Of

- We use *much* with singular (noncount) nouns and *many* with plurals. In questions, we use *how many* with plurals and *how much* with singular (noncount) nouns.
- We use *a lot of* and *lots of* with both singular (noncount) nouns and plural nouns. They are common in an informal style. They mean the same.

Q: Do you drink **much** coffee?

Q: **How much** coffee do you drink?

A: Not much. About two cups.

Q: Does he have **a lot of** (= many) friends?

Q: **How many** friends does he have?

A: Not many. About four.

	Affirmative	Negative	Questions
Count Nouns	There are **many** apples.	There aren't **many** apples.	**How many** apples are there?
	There are **a lot of** eggs.	There aren't **a lot of** eggs.	**How many** eggs are there?
	He reads **lots of** books.	He doesn't read **lots of** books.	**How many** books does he read?
Noncount Nouns	There is **much** milk.	There isn't **much** milk.	**How much** milk is there?
	There is **a lot of** food.	There isn't **a lot of** food.	**How much** food is there?
	She drinks **lots of** water.	She doesn't drink **lots of** water.	**How much** water does she drink?

Ⓐ Complete the sentences using *many*, *much*, *how many*, or *how much*.

1. There isn't __much__ snow on the roof.

2. Do you drink _____ orange juice?

3. _____ eggs are there in the fridge?

4. Peter doesn't eat _____ meat.

5. _____ information do you have?

6. She takes _____ vitamins every day.

Ⓑ Complete the sentences with *a lot of* + one of these:

| traffic | fun things | books | accidents |

1. I like to read. I have _____ *a lot of books* _____.

2. This road is very dangerous. There are _____.

3. We enjoyed our vacation. We had _____.

4. It took me a long time to drive here. There was _____.

A Use the prompts to write sentences with *some* and *any* as in the example.

1. strawberries / in the fridge ⇒ apples (X)

   → *There are some strawberries in the fridge, but there aren't any apples.*

2. milk / in the fridge ⇒ yogurt (X)

   → _____

3. tomatoes / on the table ⇒ potatoes (X)

   → _____

4. ice cream / in the fridge ⇒ chocolate (X)

   → _____

5. oranges / in the bag ⇒ carrots (X)

   → _____

B Rewrite each sentence with *every*.

1. All the waiters speak excellent Korean. → *Every waiter speaks excellent Korean.*

2. All the cooks wear uniform. → _____

3. All the children like to play. → _____

4. All the dishes come with a salad. → _____

5. All the rooms have a balcony. → _____

6. All the rooms have a bathroom. → _____

7. All the tourists have a travel guide. → _____

8. All the meals include dessert. → _____

C The underlined words are incorrect. Correct and rewrite the sentences.

I. She drinks a <u>piece</u> of milk. She doesn't drink <u>some</u> coffee.

→ *She drinks a glass of milk. She doesn't drink any coffee.*

2. Q: How <u>many</u> bread is there? A: There are two <u>bottles</u> of bread.

→ Q: _____

A: _____

3. How <u>much</u> teaspoons of sugar do you take in your tea?

→ _____

4. I ate three <u>cartons</u> of cake yesterday.

→ _____

5. Q: How <u>many</u> orange juice is there? A: There are three <u>slices</u> of orange juice.

→ Q: _____

A: _____

D Change *a lot of* to *many* or *much* in the following sentences.

I. I don't have a lot of money. → *I don't have much money.*

2. There are a lot of signs on the road. → _____

3. I don't put a lot of sugar in my tea. → _____

4. Do you have a lot of friends? → _____

5. Seoul has a lot of skyscrapers. → _____

6. I want to visit a lot of cities in Korea. → _____

7. Did they ask you a lot of questions? → _____

8. Does Jane usually buy a lot of fruit? → _____

9. Tiffany doesn't drink a lot of coffee. → _____

A Look at the example and practice with a partner. Use the words below or invent your own. (Then change roles and practice again.)

I.

 How much milk do you drink a day?

 I drink three glasses of milk.

| 1. drink milk / → three | 2. drink coffee / → four | 3. drink orange juice / → five | 4. eat pizza / → two |

5.

 Is there any bread in the basket?　　 Yes, there is some bread.

 How many sandwiches are there on the cutting board?　　 There are two sandwiches.

| 5. bread / in the basket? sandwiches / on the cutting board? → two | 6. cheese / on the plate? crackers / on the plate → four | 7. lettuce / in the fridge? tomatoes / in the fridge → two | 8. pizza / on the plate pieces of pizza / on the plate → three |

B Work with a partner. You are the grocer and your partner is the customer. Look at the pictures and act out similar dialogs.

A: Hello! What can I do for you?
B: Yes please. I need some bread with a carton of milk.
A: Here you are.
B: Thank you.

A **Write *a*, *an*, or *some*. Which nouns are count/noncount?**

1. ___a___ cookie → count / noncount   2. _____ tea → count / noncount

3. _____ armchair → count / noncount   4. _____ salt → count / noncount

5. _____ paper → count / noncount   6. _____ carrot → count / noncount

B **Write how many you can see in the pictures.**

1.

two cups of coffee

2.

_____

3.

_____

4.

_____

5.

_____

6.

_____

C **Complete the sentences with the correct form of *be going to* + base verb.**

1. Mary _____is going to make_____ (make) plans for the future.

2. Tiffany _____ (study) nursing.

3. We _____ (graduate) from the university.

4. Kevin and Jane _____ (become) US citizens.

5. She _____ (not / return) to her country.

D **Underline and correct the mistakes.**

1. How <u>many</u> sugar is there in your coffee?   →   much

2. There are any books on the table.   →   _____

3. Are there some cherries in the basket?   →   _____

4. How many coffee do you drink?   →   _____

5. How much hours do you study every day?   →   _____

E Rewrite each sentence with *every*.

1. All the rooms have a balcony. → *Every room has a balcony.*

2. All the students worked hard. → _____

3. All the students speak excellent Korean. → _____

4. All the tourists have a travel guide. → _____

F William is going to Seoul on a business trip. Write questions and give answers as in the example. Use the present progressive.

1. 8:00   Arrive in Seoul

what time / arrive / in Seoul?

Q: *What time is he arriving in Seoul?*

A: *He's arriving in Seoul at 8:00.*

2. 9:00   Meet Susan at the office

who / meet / at 9:00?

Q: _____

A: _____

3. 12:00-2:00   Have lunch with his boss

what / do / between 12:00 and 2:00?

Q: _____

A: _____

G Use the given verbs to complete the sentences. Give a future meaning to the sentences.

1. get / be

If the bus ____*is*____ late, I ____*will get*____ to work late again.

2. get / graduate

After she _____ from university, she _____ a good job.

3. ask / answer

When the interviewer _____ questions, he _____ all of them.

4. go / have

She _____ to learn Chinese if she _____ to China.

H Put in *many* or *much*.

1. She doesn't speak ___*much*___ English.

2. She doesn't buy _____ clothes.

3. I don't have _____ time.

4. There aren't _____ people here.

5. We don't have _____ rain in summer.

6. Have you traveled to _____ countries?

- Read and answer the questions.
1. What time does Jessica get up in the morning?
2. What does she do before breakfast?
3. What time do you go to bed?
4. Do you do exercise in the evening?

Unit *Focus*

▶ Prepositions of Time: *At, In, On*
▶ Prepositions of Time: *Before, After, For, During, Until, From...To*

Jessica gets up **at** seven o'clock **in the morning**. She brushes her teeth **before** breakfast. She has breakfast **at** eight o'clock **in the morning**. She goes shopping **on** Saturday afternoons. She usually watches TV **until** 11 p.m. Then, she goes to bed.

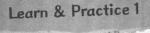 **Learn & Practice 1**

Prepositions of Time: *At, In, On*

- We use prepositions of time to say when something happens, happened, or will happen. The most common ones are *at*, *in*, and *on*. Prepositions are always followed by nouns.

Olivia usually goes to bed **at** 10 o'clock **in** the evening.

Our summer vacation begins **in** July.

We're having a party **on** Christmas Day.

At		In		On	
the time:	at 6 o'clock at 10:00 a.m. at lunchtime	**months:**	in January/February/March...	**days:**	on Monday on Christmas Day on New Year's Day on the weekend (= on weekends)
holidays:	at Christmas at Easter	**years:** **seasons:**	in 1999, in 2010 in (the) winter/spring/summer/fall		
in the expressions:	at night at midnight at the moment at noon at present at dawn	**centuries:** **in the expressions:**	in the 20th century in the morning/afternoon/evening	**dates:** **part of a particular day:** **adjective + day:**	on May 6th on Friday morning on Saturday night on a cold day

- We can use *in* for a future time measured from the present.
  E.g. Don't go anywhere. I'll be back **in** ten minutes. The building will open **in** six weeks.

A Write *at, in,* or *on.*

1. ___in___ December

2. _____ the morning

3. _____ 12:00

4. _____ night

5. _____ the evening

6. _____ 2018

7. _____ Christmas Day

8. _____ a cold evening

9. _____ March

10. _____ Saturday afternoon

B Fill in the blanks with the prepositions of time: *at, in,* or *on.*

1.

I usually go to bed __at__ 10 p.m.

2.

My friend plays basketball _____ Mondays and Fridays.

3.

We go to the beach _____ summer.

4.

We celebrate Christmas _____ December 25th.

5.

My parents went to Paris _____ 2011.

6.

This store closes _____ lunchtime.

C Fill in the blanks with the correct form of the words in brackets. Put the correct prepositions in the boxes.

1. Where ___does Bob go___ (Bob / go) | on | the weekend?

2. My sisters _____ (not play) soccer | | Sundays.

3. _____ (you / often / hang) out with your friends | | the afternoon?

4. What time _____ (Carly / have) lunch | | weekdays?

Prepositions of Time: *Before, After, For, During, Until, From...To*

- We use *for* and *during* to say how long something has continued. We use *for* (not during) + a period of time (three days / two years / four months, etc.)
- We use *before* and *after* to say when something happens.

I went home **after** the movie.

I fell asleep **for** 2 hours in the movie theater.

before the movie **during** the movie

- We use *until (= till)* to say when an action or situation ends.
- We use *from...to* to give the beginning and end of an action or situation.

John waited for Jane **until** 9 o'clock.

We lived in Korea **from** 1999 **to** 2002.

A Write *before, after, until,* or *from*.

1. Wash your hands __before__ dinner.
2. Everybody is nervous _____ exams.
3. I work _____ Monday to Friday.
4. I waited for her _____ 11 o'clock.
5. _____ World War II, people tried to keep the peace.
6. New Year's Day is _____ Christmas.

B Write *for* or *during*.

1. They didn't speak __during__ the meal.
2. Kevin studied in Hong Kong _____ three years.
3. I learned yoga _____ the weekend.
4. I usually watch TV _____ two hours in the evening.
5. We stayed in Rome _____ five days.
6. We visited Tokyo _____ the holiday.
7. They lived in Seattle _____ three years.
8. They swim every day _____ the summer.

A Complete the sentences. Each time use *at*, *in*, or *on* with one of the words or phrases from the box below.

| April 11th | July 21, 1969 | the 15th century | night | 10 o'clock |

1. Columbus discovered America _____ *in the 15th century* _____.

2. Q: Do you know your daughter's birthday? A: Yes, it's _____.

3. You can see the stars _____ if the sky is clear.

4. Q: What time did you leave home? A: I left home _____.

5. The first man landed on the moon _____.

B Rewrite the sentences with prepositions of time.

1.

Janet finished high school. (2005)

→ *Jane finished high school in 2005.*

2.

We have class. (ten to eleven)

→ _____

3.

The family restaurant closes. (10:00 p.m.)

→ _____

4.

I'll wait for Susan. (7 o'clock)

→ _____

5.

I always feel tired. (the morning)

→ _____

6.

My husband and I fell asleep. (the movie)

→ _____

C Make sentences with *in*.

1. It's 3 o'clock now. The plane leaves at 5:00.

   → The plane leaves in two hours. _____

2. It's 5:25 now. The train leaves at 5:30.

   → _____

3. It's Monday today. I'll call you on Thursday.

   → _____

4. It's 2 o'clock now. Jason will be here at 6:00.

   → _____

D Read the questions and answer them as in the example.

1. Q: What time does the bank open?   A: It opens at 8:00 a.m. _____ (8:00 a.m.)

2. Q: What time does Kathy leave home? A: _____ (9 o'clock)

3. Q: When is New Year's Day?   A: _____ (January 1st)

4. Q: When is Valentine's Day?   A: _____ (February 14th)

5. Q: When does he go on vacation?   A: _____ (winter)

E Read the information and make sentences with *for* and *until*, as in the example.

1.
Katie

I lived in Korea since 2002.
I came to Japan in 2005.

Katie lived in Korea for three
years.

She lived in Korea until
2005.

2.
Cindy

I lived in Canada since 2006.
I came to Korea in 2011.

_____
_____
_____
_____

3.
Wilson

I lived in China since 1999.
I came to England in 2008.

_____
_____
_____
_____

A Look at the example and practice with a partner. Use the words below or invent your own. (Then change roles and practice again.)

I.

What time do you leave for school?

I leave for school at seven o'clock in the morning.

I.
what time / leave for school?
→ seven o'clock / the morning

2.
when / play soccer?
→ Sundays

3.
what time / do your homework?
→ four o'clock / the afternoon

4.
when / go snowboarding?
→ usually / Saturday afternoon

5.
what time / wake up?
→ 6 o'clock / the morning

6.
when / have English class?
→ Tuesday mornings

B Work with a partner. Read the information and describe the three people as in the example.

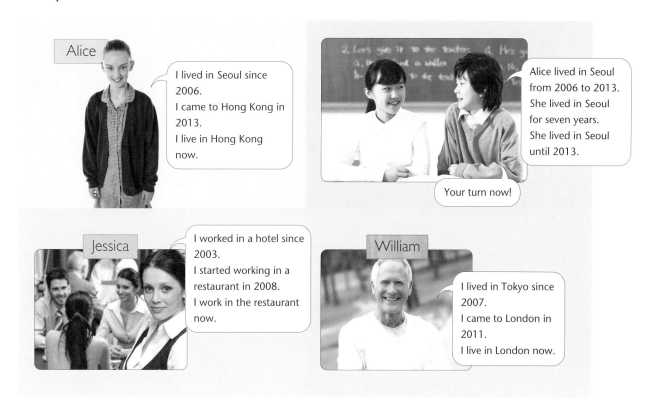

Alice

I lived in Seoul since 2006.
I came to Hong Kong in 2013.
I live in Hong Kong now.

Alice lived in Seoul from 2006 to 2013.
She lived in Seoul for seven years.
She lived in Seoul until 2013.

Your turn now!

Jessica

I worked in a hotel since 2003.
I started working in a restaurant in 2008.
I work in the restaurant now.

William

I lived in Tokyo since 2007.
I came to London in 2011.
I live in London now.

Prepositions of Place and Movement

• Read and answer the questions.
1. Where is Brian's house? Draw the route.
2. Where is the bank?
3. Where is the Italian restaurant?

cafe	candy store				bookstore
			GAVIN STREET		
	clothes shop		newsdealer's	shoe store	
Chinese restaurant	Italian restaurant		shopping center	supermarket	police station
		GLENN STREET	BRAXTON AVENUE		
cafe	theater		movie theater		library
art gallery	museum		hotel	bank	
Start ★			SMITHSON AVENUE		
	train station		park		

Dear Bob,

I'm afraid I can't pick you up from the station on Friday. But my house isn't far from there. Here are the directions: When you get out of the station, turn right and walk along Smithson Avenue. Turn left at the museum into Glenn Street. Go up the street and at the newsdealer's turn right into Gavin Street. My house is at number 32, next to a shoe store and opposite a bookstore. I'm sending you a map too, so you can't miss it!

Brian

Unit Focus

▶ Prepositions of Place
▶ Prepositions of Movement

Learn & Practice 1

Prepositions of Place

- We use prepositions of place to say where somebody or something is.

 **at** the door

 **at** the bus stop

 **at** home

 on the box

 **in** the box

 **under** the tree

 **on** the horse

 **next to (= by)** the dog

 behind the door

 **in front of** the bus

 The picture is **above** the bed.

 **near** the river

 opposite the girl/boy

 **above** the clouds

 The kids are **between** their mom **and** dad.

 The sofa is **below** the picture.

 My family is having a barbecue **in front of** my house. My dad is cooking **opposite** us.

A Look at the pictures and fill in the blanks with the correct prepositions.

1.
Donald's standing __next__ __to / by__ the window.

2.
The vases are _____ the table.

3.
They're standing _____ _____ the Eiffel Tower.

4.
Henry is _____ Kevin and David.

5.
Laura is _____ the airport.

6.
The picture is _____ the sofa.

Prepositions of Movement

- We use prepositions of movement to show the direction in which somebody or something is moving.

They're running **to** school.

She's running **up** the hill.

They're running **down** the hill.

They're jumping **into** the pool.

The car's going **through** the tunnel.

He's walking **across** the street.

He's jumping **our of** the window.

He's driving **along** the road.

He's climbing **onto** the roof.

She's driving **from** London **to** Brighton.

He's riding his tricycle **around** the house.

Prepositions of Place and Movement **93**

A Choose the correct prepositions and put them in the correct places.

1.

(along / across / over)

The plane is flying ___over___ the city.
The car is going ___along___ the street.
The man is walking ___across___ the street.

2.

(out of / into)

The man is getting _____ the taxi.
The woman is getting _____ the taxi.

3.

(down / up)

Tom is going _____ the hill.
Cindy is going _____ the hill.

4.

(from...to / through)

The bus is going _____ the tunnel.
The bus is going _____ London _____ Oxford.

B Read and choose a preposition.

1. The students ran (into / through / out) the classroom quickly when the teacher arrived.

2. The cat climbed (across / up / along) the tree and didn't come down.

3. Look! They baby is walking (out of / into / across) the street.

4. Bob and Peter are cycling (around / down / up) the park.

5. We walked (to / out of / from) the hotel to the restaurant.

6. I took the old batteries (into / onto / out of) the radio.

7. Be careful! You may fall (up / down / along) the stairs.

8. A bird flew into the room (into / through / across) a window.

9. She was walking (onto / through / along) the street with her dog.

Ⓐ Answer the questions. Use *at/in/on* + the words in parentheses.

1.

(the balcony)

Q: Where is she standing?

A: *On the balcony.*

2.

(the bus stop)

Q: Where are they?

A: _____

3.

(the airport)

Q: Where is Kiara?

A: _____

4.

(the wall)

Q: Where is the clock?

A: _____

5.

(the bus)

Q: Where are they?

A: _____

6.

(the table)

Q: Where is the woman?

A: _____

Ⓑ Look at the map and complete each sentence with the name of a place.

1. The school is next to _____the bank_____.

2. The KFC is next to _____.

3. The record shop is opposite _____.

4. _____ is between the shoe store and the post office.

5. The restaurant is across from _____.

6. The record shop is between _____ and _____.

school	bank		flower shop
	KFC		
hospital	record shop		shoe store
	bookstore		restaurant
			post office

C Look at the pictures and correct the mistakes.

1.
The cars will go <u>down</u> the tunnel. → _through_

2.
Many people are walking <u>out of</u> the street. → _____

3.
They're walking <u>up</u> the forest path. → _____

4.
The athlete ran <u>between</u> Paris to Brussels. → _____

5.
She is getting <u>around</u> the bus. → _____

D Answer the questions according to the map.

John Kennedy St.	Record Shop	Travel Agency	George Washington St.	Disco	Video Shop	Lincoln Street
					Pizza Bar	
	Snack Bar	Supermarket		Museum	Library	
	Thomas Jefferson			Avenue		
	Movie Theater	Church		Post Office	Hospital	
	Bookstore	Sports Goods Store		Flower Shop	Drugstore	
	Shoe Store					

1. You're on George Washington St. Is the disco opposite the supermarket?
   → No, it isn't. It is opposite the travel agency.

2. You're on Lincoln St. Is the drugstore behind the hospital?
   → _____

3. You're on John Kennedy St. Is the bookstore between the church and the sports goods store?
   → _____

4. You're on Thomas Jefferson Avenue. Is the post office across from the hospital?
   → _____

A Look at the example and practice with a partner. Use the words below or invent your own. (Then change roles and practice again.)

I.

Is there a woman in front of the fence?

No, there isn't. She is behind the fence.

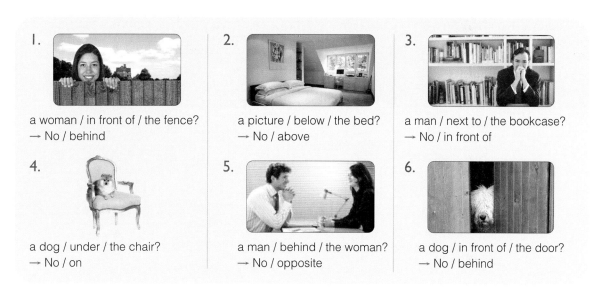

1.
a woman / in front of / the fence?
→ No / behind

2.
a picture / below / the bed?
→ No / above

3.
a man / next to / the bookcase?
→ No / in front of

4.
a dog / under / the chair?
→ No / on

5.
a man / behind / the woman?
→ No / opposite

6.
a dog / in front of / the door?
→ No / behind

B Work with a partner. Look at the map below. Choose a place. Your partner must guess where you are.

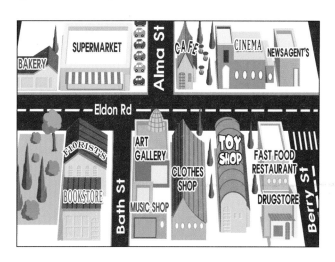

I'm on Berry St. It's next to the drugstore.

You're at the fast food restaurant.

Your turn now.

Prepositions of Place and Movement 97

- Read and answer the questions.
1. Do you have to wear a school uniform?
2. Can you bring your smartphone to class?
3. What are your school rules?

*U*nit *F*ocus

▶ *Can, Could*
▶ *Should*
▶ *Must* vs. *Have To*

What are the rules at school?
- You can bring your cell phone to school.
- You shouldn't use your phone in class.
- You have to wear a school uniform.
- You have to be quiet in class.
- You mustn't run in the hallway.
- You don't have to bring your lunch.

Learn & Practice 1

Can, Could

- We use *can* or *can't (= cannot)* to talk about ability or permission in the present.
- We use *could* or *couldn't (= could not)* to talk about ability or permission in the past.

Ability		Permission	

Our dog is amazing. It **can** sing!	Michelle **could** play basketball last year, but she **can't** play basketball now.	You **can't** talk in the library.	I **could** use the laptop at home.

Affirmative

I		
You	**can**	swim.
He/She/It	**could**	go.
We		
They		

Negative

I		
You	**can't** (cannot)	swim.
He/She/It	**couldn't** (could not)	go.
We		
They		

Questions

	I	
Can	you	run?
Could	he/she/it	swim?
	we	
	they	

Short Answers

Yes, I **can**. / No, I **can't**.
Yes, you **can**. / No, you **can't**.
Yes, he/she/it **can**. / No, he/she/it **can't**.
Yes, we **could**. / No, we **couldn't**.
Yes, they **can**. / No, they **can't**.

A Complete the sentences with *can*, *can't*, *could*, or *couldn't*.

1. She ___could___ play the piano when she was five.

2. Fred _____ dive and swim very well.

3. I was tired, but I _____ sleep.

B Make questions for each answer using the prompts below.

1. you / write with your left hand?
   → Q: *Can you write with your left hand?* _____   A: No, I can't.

2. Jane / eat with chopsticks?
   → Q: _____   A: Yes, she can.

3. you / speak English / when you were younger?
   → Q: _____   A: No, I couldn't.

Learn & Practice 2

Should

- We use *should* to give someone advice. *Should* means it's a good idea to do something.
- We use *shouldn't (= should not)* when it's a bad idea to do something.

You **should** study hard for your finals.
(= I think studying hard is the right thing
   for you to do.)

They **shouldn't** eat so many candies.
(= I think eating a lot of candies is the
   wrong thing for them to do.)

Subject	Should	Base Verb	Yes/No Question
I/We/You He/She/It They/Tom, etc.	should / shouldn't	go.	Q: **Should** I go there? A: **Yes**, you **should**. **No**, you **shouldn't**.

A Fill in the blanks with *should* or *shouldn't*.

1. Wilson looks exhausted. He ___shouldn't___ work so hard.

2. A: I need to lose weight. What _____ I do?

   B: You _____ join an aerobics class. It's a great way to keep fit.

Must vs. *Have To*

- We use *must, have/has to* to tell someone to do something.
- We use *have to* for something that is necessary. But *have to* is not as strong as *must*. We use *must* for rules or strong advice. When we use *must*, we have no choice.

You **must** listen to me carefully.　　She **has to** study for the test.　　**Does** Clara **have to** finish the project tomorrow?

- We use *must not (= mustn't)* to tell someone not to do something. We use *must not* when something is against the law or rules or it isn't right.
- We use *don't/doesn't have to* to say that something is not necessary. There is a choice.

I **must go** to the bank. I have no more money. (It's a necessity, there is no other choice.)　　You **mustn't** park here. (It's against the law or rules.)　　Tomorrow is Sunday. We **don't have to** get up early.

- We use *do/does...have to?* to ask if something is necessary.
  E.g. Q: **Do** we **have to** go to school tomorrow?　A: Yes, you do. / No, you don't have to.

Ⓐ Complete the sentences with the words in brackets.

1. I'm late for the meeting. I ____*have to run*____ (run / have to).

2. Scott _____ (wear / have to) a suit for his new job.

3. You _____ (clean / must) your room right now!

4. _____ (we / work / have to) on Saturday?

5. It's raining. You _____ (go out / not must) without your umbrella.

A Rewrite the sentences using *must* or *must not.*

1. Don't talk in the library.
   → You must not talk in the library.

2. It is very important for me to study hard for this exam.
   →

3. It is very important for children to drink lots of milk.
   →

4. Don't stay in the sun for a long time.
   →

5. It is necessary for them to be here at 9 o'clock.
   →

6. It is very important that students do not leave school early without permission.
   →

B Look at the pictures and prompts. Write questions and answers using *have to.*

1.
Sunny / work / in the afternoon?
→ No / in the morning

Q: Does Sunny have to work in the
afternoon?

A: No, she doesn't. She has to work in the
morning.

2.
Mary / study / history tonight?
→ No / geography

Q:

A:

3.
they / wash the car every day?
→ No / on the weekend

Q:

A:

4.
Jessica / go to the doctor / today?
→ No / tomorrow

Q:

A:

C Look at the pictures and cues. What can/could they do? Write sentences as in the example.

1.

Now

Past

Lisa: drive a car   ride a bicycle

Lisa can drive a car now. When she was younger, she could only ride a bicycle.

2.

Now

Past

Jack: play golf   play soccer

_____

_____

3.

Now

Past

Wilson: ride a snowboard   ride a skateboard

_____

_____

D Write four things you couldn't do before, but you can do now.

1. Six years ago, I couldn't sing, but I can sing well now.

2. _____

3. _____

4. _____

5. _____

E Read the situations. Then use the prompts to write sentences giving advice. Use *should* or *shouldn't*.

1. Kathy wants to lose weight.   → She should do exercise more.   (do exercise / more)

   → She shouldn't eat candies.   (eat / candies)

2. Jessica feels very tired.   → _____   (take / a break)

   → _____   (work / so hard)

3. Steve can never wake up early   → _____   (use / an alarm clock)

   in the morning, so he's always   → _____   (go / to bed / late / at night)

   late for school.

A Look at the example and practice with a partner. Use the words below or invent your own. (Then change roles and practice again.)

1.

 Why do I have to go to the flower shop?

 You have to buy some flowers.

1.

go to the flower shop?
→ buy some flowers

2.

go to the supermarket?
→ get some milk

3.

go to the post office?
→ mail a package

4.

stay home tonight?
→ do your homework

5.

go downtown?
→ buy some new clothes

6.

go to the bookstore?
→ buy some books

B Work with a partner. Make sentences using *should* or *shouldn't* for the following situations. Use some of the verbs and expressions given.

smoke

touch the statues

use your hands to eat

make a lot of noise

ear or drink inside

study

use your cell phone

wear your seatbelt

When you are in a library, you should be quiet.

When you are in a library, you shouldn't eat.

Your turn now!

when you're in a library

when you're on an airplane

when you're in a restaurant

when you're in a museum

Helping Verbs 2

• Read and answer the questions.
1. What is he doing now?
2. Could he be late for the meeting?
3. Has he got lost on the way?

Unit Focus

▶ *May/Might/Can/Could* to Express Possibility
▶ *May/Could/Can I* to Ask for Permission
▶ *Would/Could/Can You* to Make Requests
▶ *Must* to Make Deductions

A: There's a lot of traffic I may/might/could be a little late for the meeting. Where's Jane?

B: I don't know, but she must be in the bookstore. She said she might buy a book.

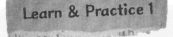

May, Might, Can, and Could to Express Possibility

- We use *may, might, can,* or *could* to express possibility in the present or future. May, might, can, and could mean "perhaps." We can use *can* in affirmative sentences when we talk about a more general possibility of something happening.

That's dangerous! She **may/might/could** fall!
(= Perhaps she will fall.)

The temperature **can** sometimes reach 35℃ in July.

- We don't use *may* to ask questions about the possibility of something happening. *Might* can be used in *yes/no* questions, but it is very formal.

Sunny doesn't drive carefully.
Could she have an accident?
Might she have an accident? (very formal)
~~**May** she have an accident?~~ (X)

Subject	Modal (+ *Not*)	Base Verb
I/We/You He/She/It They/Tom, etc.	may may not might might not could	go.

* We do not contract *may* and *might* with *not*.
* We do not use *could* in the **negative**.

E.g. The rumor **may/might not** be true.
~~The rumor **could not** be true.~~ (X)

A Read the underlined words and write *possibility*, *ability*, or *permission*.

1. Some jobs <u>can</u> be very tiring.   →   *possibility*

2. David <u>could</u> play the guitar.   →   _____

3. You <u>may</u> come into the computer room.   →   _____

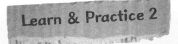

May I, Could I, and Can I to Ask for Permission

- We use *may I*, *could I*, and *can I* to ask for permission to do something. *May I* is the most polite or formal of the three. *Could I* is more polite or formal than *can I*. We use *can I* when we know the other person very well.

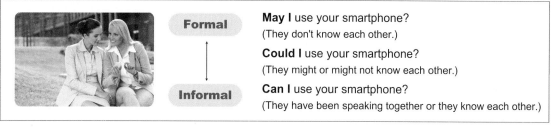

Formal	**May I** use your smartphone? (They don't know each other.)	
↕	**Could I** use your smartphone? (They might or might not know each other.)	
Informal	**Can I** use your smartphone? (They have been speaking together or they know each other.)	

- We usually say *Okay*; *Yes, of course*; *Certainly*; *Sure*; *No problem*; *I'm sorry, but...*; *No, I'm sorry*; *No, thanks*.

A Complete the conversations with *may I*, *could I*, or *can I*.

1. A: ____Can I____ have another napkin? B: Sure. (They know each other.)

2. A: _____ see your driver's licence? B: Yes, of course. (They don't know each other.)

3. A: _____ use your computer? B: Certainly. (They might or might not know each other.)

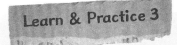

Would You, Could You, and Can You to Make Requests

- We can ask people to do something with *would you*, *could you*, and *can you*. We generally use *would* and *could* when we make requests of strangers, older people, teachers, or bosses. We use *can* with friends and family members.

Would/Could you call me later?   **Can you** lend me a pen?

* We usually say ***Certainly***; ***Sure***; ***Yes, of course***; ***OK***; ***Sorry, I can't***; ***I'd like to, but I....***

A Find better ways of asking people to do these things. (I = informal, P = polite)

1. Open the window. (I)   *Can you open the window?*

2. Open the door. (P)   *Would/Could you open the door?*

3. Turn down the volume. (I)   _____

4. Get me a glass of cold water. (P)   _____

5. Tell me the time. (P)   _____

6. Watch my children for a minute. (I)   _____

Learn & Practice 4

Must to Make Deductions

- We use *must* when we believe that something is true. *Must* expresses what is logical in the situation.

A: Who is that woman? Is she a student?
B: I don't know, but I've seen her go into the classroom.
A: Oh, she **must be** a teacher. She **must not** be a student.

She **is** a teacher. (100% certainty)
She **must be** a teacher. (95% certainty)
She **may/might/could be** a teacher. (less than 50% certainty)

A Complete the sentences with *must* or *must not* and the verbs in brackets.

1. Marilyn worked for ten hours today. She _____*must be*_____ (be) tired.

2. Jennifer can take the bus everywhere. She _____ (have) a car.

3. The phone rang eight times and Cindy didn't answer. She _____ (be) at home.

4. The girls are playing in the hot sun for an hour. They _____ (be) thirsty.

5. It's the most popular restaurant in town, so the food _____ (be) good.

6. Somebody is knocking on the door. It _____ (be) Olivia. She went to a movie this afternoon.

7. Jessica wears something blue every day. She _____ (like) the color blue.

A Write requests using *Can I/you...?* or *Could I/you...? Can* and *could* are both correct in each sentence.

1. I want to have a drink.

   → Can I have a drink?

   → Could I have a drink?

2. I want you to open the door.

   → Can you open the door?

   → Could you open the door?

3. I want you to answer the phone.

   → _____

   → _____

4. I want to turn on the television.

   → _____

   → _____

5. I want you to help me with my suitcase.

   → _____

   → _____

6. I want to borrow this book.

   → _____

   → _____

B Look at the pictures. Use the following phrases to complete the sentences expressing possibility. Use *may*, *might*, or *could*.

become an astronaut	be at the library	win the race
sell his new car	become famous	visit him tomorrow

1.

   Brian needs some money, so he <u>may/might/could</u> <u>sell his new car</u>.

2.

   Susan is crazy about space. She _____.

3.

   Karen is a great artist, so she _____.

4.
   Lisa runs very fast, so she _____.

5.

   I want to see my best friend, so I _____.

6.
   Mary isn't at home now. She _____.

C Rewrite the sentences in italics using *must* or *must not*.

1. His light's out. *I'm sure he's not at home.* → He must not be at home.

2. Anna finally got a job. *I'm sure she's happy.* → She must be happy.

3. Listen to her accent. *She is certainly not American.* → _____

4. She has a very expensive car. *I'm sure she's rich.* → _____

5. The phone's ringing. I know it's not for me. *I'm sure it is for you.* → _____

6. My keys aren't in the living room. *I am sure they're in the kitchen.* → _____

7. He's very bad-tempered. *I feel sure he doesn't have many friends.* → _____

D Write four things that you might do tomorrow.

1. I might go to the movies tomorrow. _____

2. _____

3. _____

4. _____

5. _____

E Read the situations. Make questions with *may I*, *can I*, or *could you*, as in the example.

1. You are a teenager. You want to go to a party tonight. Ask your mom.
   → Can I go to a party tonight? _____

2. You want to invite some friends to dinner. What do you say to your mother?
   → _____

3. You're an attendant at the theater. You want to see a person's ticket.
   → _____

4. You want your teacher to open the door for you. What do you say?
   → _____

5. Tom wants his father to teach him how to drive a car. What does he say?
   → _____

A Look at the example and practice with a partner. Use the words below or invent your own. (Then change roles and practice again.)

1.

 I can't find Kathy. Have you seen her?

 She might be in the tennis court. She may be playing tennis now.

1.

Kathy / ?
→ in the tennis court /
play tennis now

2.

Vanessa / ?
→ in the music room /
play the guitar now

3.

Emily / ?
→ in the library /
study now

4.

David / ?
→ at home /
watch TV now

5.

Tina / ?
→ in the restaurant /
have lunch now

6.

Jack / ?
→ in his room /
do his homework
now

B Work with a partner. Ask and answer polite questions using *may I*, *could I*, or *can I*.

1. You want to use a grammar book.
   Your partner has it.

2. You want to use a laptop.
   Your partner has it.

3. You want to borrow a dictionary.
   Your partner has it.

4. You want to use an eraser.
   Your partner has it.

5. You want to borrow a cell phone.
   Your partner has it.

6. You want to use a calculator.
   Your partner has it.

May I use your grammar book?

No problem. Here it is.

Thank you. Your turn now.

A Choose the correct words.

1. The post office is _____ the shopping center and the museum.

   a. front of   b. next   c. between.

2. The bus stop is _____ of the police station.

   a. behind   b. in front   c. opposite

3. The students ran _____ the classroom quickly when the teacher arrived.

   a. out   b. through   c. into

4. The cat climbed _____ the tree and didn't come down.

   a. along   b. up   c. across

5. There is a shoe store _____ to the movie theater.

   a. behind   b. opposite   c. next

6. Look! The baby is walking _____ the street.

   a. across   b. above   c. out of

B Read the situations. Make questions with *may I* or *can I* as in the example.

1. You want to borrow your friend's camera. What do you say to him?

   → *Can I borrow your camera?* _____

2. You want to use the phone in your boss's office. What do you say to him?

   → _____

3. Your brother has a dictionary. You want to borrow it. What do you say to him?

   → _____

4. You are at a restaurant. You want to have a cup of coffee. What do you say to a waiter/waitres

   → _____

C Use the prompts to make sentences about Peter's Sunday morning, as in the example. Use *from...to.*

1. read the newspaper / 7:00 / 8:00   *He read the newspaper from 7:00 to 8:00.*

2. washed his car / 9:00 / 10:00   _____

3. played tennis / 11:00 / 12:00   _____

4. talked to his friends / 12:00 / 1:00   _____

D Complete the sentences using *you should* or *you shouldn't* and a verb from the box. A verb may be used more than once.

drink   eat   smoke   take

How to Stay Healthy

1. _You should eat_ a lot of fresh fruit and vegetables.

2. _____ too many candies.
3. _____ regular exercise.

4. _____ any cigarettes.
5. _____ too much coffee.

E Read the situations and write sentences from the words in brackets. Use *must*.

1. The cat is ill. (you / take it / to the vet)   →   _You must take it to the vet._

2. Kelly has a headache. (she / take / an aspirin)   →   _____

3. The milk smells bad. (you / not / drink it)   →   _____

4. The water is dirty. (you / not / swim here)   →   _____

F Fill in the blanks with the prepositions of time, *at*, *in*, or *on*.

1. School starts _____ September.

2. She usually goes shopping _____ Saturdays.

3. We can get to the city center _____ 10 minutes.

4. We're meeting _____ 10:00.

G Write full sentences, as in the example. Use a polite question with *Would/Could you...?*

1. It's getting hot in here. _____ _Would/Could you open the window?_ _____ (open / the window)

2. The phone is ringing, but my hands are full.
_____ (answer / the phone)

3. I'm trying to study, but the music is too loud.
_____ (turn down / the volume)

H Circle the correct answers.

1. Jessica had a big lunch, so she (might want / might not want) to eat this evening.

2. If the traffic gets very bad, we (might miss / might not miss) the train.

3. Isabella's not feeling well today. I'm afraid she (might pass / might not pass) her exam.

4. Alice wasn't at the last meeting. She (might know / might not know) the new members.

Unit 17 Infinitives

• Read and answer the questions.
1. Why did she go to a coffee shop?
2. Do you like to read fantasy books?
3. What is your favorite book?

Unit Focus

▶ Verb + Infinitive
▶ Verb + Object + Infinitive
▶ Infinitive of Purpose

From an early age, J. K. Rowling wanted to become a great writer. She was very poor. She went to a coffee shop to write the Harry Potter books. Later her books became very popular. Children and adults went to a bookstore to buy them.

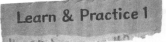
Learn & Practice 1

Verb + Infinitive

- An infinitive (*to* + base verb) acts like a noun in a sentence.
- Like a noun or a pronoun, we use an infinitive as an object of certain verbs and constructions.

Olivia decided **to teach** Korean history.

Verb		Object
want expect would like need decide plan hope promise	+	to + base verb

A Complete the sentences with the infinitive of the verbs in brackets.

1. What do you want ___to buy___ (buy)?

2. I'm very tired. I need _____ (sleep).

3. Are you planning _____ (take) a vacation this year?

4. I want _____ (meet) my grandparents.

5. Children like _____ (play) computer games.

6. I hope _____ (watch) TV in English.

7. Ryan decided _____ (study) Korean.

Learn & Practice 2

Verb + Object + Infinitive

- After certain verbs, we use the verb + an object + an infinitive.
- We often say that we want somebody to do something. We can use *would like* + an object + an infinitive in the same way.

The doctor *advised* me **to eat** more vegetables.

I *want* you **to listen** to this song. (= I'*d like* you **to listen** to this song.)

Verb			Infinitive
advise, allow, ask, encourage, order, want (= would like), persuade, permit, teach, tell, warn	+ Object +		to + base verb

A Put the words in brackets into the correct form.

1. My mother wanted ___me to finish___ (I / finish) my homework.

2. The teacher allows _____ (we / leave) early.

3. My boss told _____ (I / write) the reports before Friday.

4. I'd like _____ (you / join) my club.

5. I warned _____ (he / drive) slowly because of the bad weather.

6. Nancy didn't feel too good, but we persuaded _____ (she / come) to the party.

7. They asked _____ (their neighbors / be) quiet.

Learn & Practice 3

Infinitive of Purpose

- We use an infinitive to talk about the reason or purpose for doing something (why someone does something).
- In more formal English, we use *in order to* to explain a purpose.
- We can also use *for* to show purpose. We use a noun after *for*.

Q: Why did she go to the bookstore?
A: She went to the bookstore **to buy** some books.

She went to the cafeteria **for** lunch.

We cross our middle and index fingers **in order to** wish good luck.

Ⓐ Complete the sentences with *to* or *for*.

1. I go to the library ___to___ read some books.

2. We go to school _____ get an education.

3. Our teacher always gives us lots of exercises _____ homework.

4. We use the Internet _____ do research.

5. Our teacher sometimes uses videos _____ discussion.

Ⓑ Look at the pictures and match to complete each sentence.

1.  2.   3.   4.   5.

1. Steve went to the cafeteria •   • a. to see animals.

2. We're going to the bakery •   • b. to have some lunch.

3. They study English •   • c. to buy some milk.

4. Bob and his family went to the supermarket •   • d. to buy a cake.

5. We went to the zoo •   • e. to get a better job.

114 Unit 17

Super Writing

A Write where these people want to go and what they would like to see there.

	Paris / the Eiffel Tower	London / Big Ben	Egypt / the Pyramids	Korea / the Seoul Tower
Susan	✓			
Brian			✓	
Chris & Cindy				✓
Jason		✓		
You				

1. Susan _wants to go to Paris. She would like to see the Eiffel Tower._

2. Brian _____

3. Chris and Cindy _____

4. Jason _____

5. I _____

B Emily went to all these places yesterday. Why did she go there? Look at the pictures and use the prompts to make sentences as in the example.

1.

the train station / catch a train

→ _She went to the train station to catch a train._

2.

the library / return a book

→ _____

_____

3.

a flower shop / buy some flowers

→ _____

_____

4.

a coffee shop / meet a friend

→ _____

_____

C Rewrite the sentences using the verbs in brackets and *to*-infinitives.

1. "Stay at my house on Saturday night," Kevin said to Maria. (tell)

   → Kevin told Maria to stay at his house on Saturday night .

2. "You should see a doctor," they said to me. (advise)

   → They _____ .

3. "Turn left after the bridge," a woman said to me. (tell)

   → A woman _____ .

4. "Tidy the bedroom," Mom said to us. (order)

   → Mom _____ .

5. "Please come to my house for a barbecue on Saturday," she said to us. (invite)

   → She _____ .

6. "You should wash your feet," Helen said to Peter. (persuade)

   → Helen _____ .

D Combine the two sentences to make one sentence. Use infinitives.

1. She wants to lose weight. She wants to be the most beautiful at the party.

   → She wants to lose weight to be the most beautiful at the party.

2. John went to France. He wanted to learn French.

   → _____

3. My sister is going shopping. She is going to buy some fresh fruit.

   → _____

4. I stayed at home. I helped my mother.

   → _____

5. I learn English. I can communicate with other people.

   → _____

6. Cathy went to the store. She wanted to buy a newspaper.

   → _____

A Look at the example and practice with a partner. Use the words below or invent your own. (Then change roles and practice again.)

1.

Alice / go to the bakery?
→ buy / some bread

1.

 Why did Alice go to the bakery?

 She went to the bakery to buy some bread.

2.

Peter / go to Pizza Hut?
→ have / some pizza

3.

Scott / put on / his jogging suit?
→ go jogging

4.

Kevin / recycle / old newspapers and books?
→ protect / the environment

5.

Isabella / call Justin?
→ invite / him / to her birthday party

B Work with a partner. Tell your partner about five places you want to go to and what you would like to see there.

Paris /
the Eiffel Tower

London /
the clock tower, Big Ben

Korea /
the Seoul Tower

Australia / the Sydney
Opera House

I want to go to Korea. I would like to see the Seoul Tower.

Your turn now!

Paris / the Louvre
Museum

Rome /
the Colosseum

New York /
the Statue of Liberty

Italy / the Leaning
Tower of Pisa

Unit 18 Gerunds

• Read and answer the questions.
1. What does Andrew hate doing?
2. Do you like skiing?
3. In your free time, what do you enjoy doing?

Unit Focus

▶ Gerunds: Subject
▶ Gerunds: Object
▶ Go + -ing

Andrew: I hate staying at home every weekend. I would like to do something different this weekend.
Cindy: Let's spend the weekend at the ski resort. We can both enjoy skiing. Our children love playing in the snow.
Andrew: Great idea. Learning ski is really fun.

Learn & Practice 1

Gerunds: Subject

- To make a gerund, we add *-ing* to the base form of the verb. A gerund (v-*ing*) acts like a noun in a sentence.
- We use a noun or a pronoun as a subject. Like a noun or a pronoun, a gerund can be the subject.

Noun	**English** is an international language.
Pronoun	**It** is an international language.
Gerund	**Studying** English is very interesting.

Yoga is a popular activity for women.

Learning yoga is very interesting.

I like **learning** yoga.

Ⓐ Complete the sentences using the prompts given, as in the example.

1. _____Watching TV_____ (watch / TV) all evening is boring, let's do something else.

2. _____ (take / a good rest) is the most important thing.

3. _____ (learn / a foreign language) is important.

4. _____ (read / in a dark room) is bad for the eyes.

Gerunds: Object

- Like a noun or a pronoun, we use a gerund as the object in a sentence.
- After certain verbs, we use a gerund as the object.

We really *enjoy* **traveling** abroad.

Karen *finished* **studying** at midnight.

Verb		Object
enjoy finish give up keep mind avoid stop put off quit dislike	+	**verb + -ing**

- We can use a gerund or an infinitive after certain verbs. The meaning is the same.

She **started teaching** Korean history.
She **started to teach** Korean history.

Verb		Gerund/Infinitive
like hate love begin start continue	+	**to + base verb** *or* **verb + -ing**

Ⓐ Complete the sentences with the gerund or infinitive form of the verbs in brackets. Sometimes two answers are possible.

1. Juliet enjoys _____playing_____ (play) the guitar.

2. He started _____ (drive) when he was 18 years old.

3. I like _____ (do) my homework.

4. I wanted _____ (take) my dog to the park yesterday.

5. Bob finished _____ (paint) the picture yesterday.

6. My friends and I are planning _____ (go) camping this weekend.

7. She doesn't like _____ (sing) in front of other people.

8. Would you mind _____ (open) the window?

Go + -ing

- We use a gerund after the verb *go* to express recreational activities. There is no *to* between *go* and the gerund.

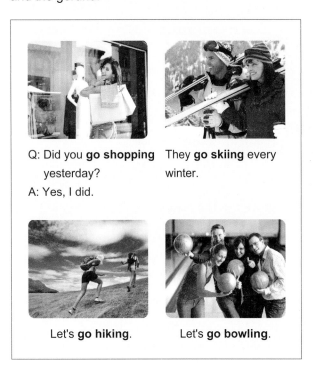

Q: Did you **go shopping** yesterday?
A: Yes, I did.

They **go skiing** every winter.

Let's **go hiking**.

Let's **go bowling**.

Go		-ing
go	+	camp**ing** fish**ing** shopp**ing** hik**ing** jogg**ing** bowl**ing** sightsee**ing** sail**ing** skat**ing** swimm**ing**

Ⓐ Make sentences with *Would you like to go...?*

1. fishing → *Would you like to go fishing?* _____
2. sailing → _____
3. skating → _____
4. sightseeing → _____
5. shopping → _____

Ⓑ Look at the pictures and complete the sentences. Use *go/goes + -ing*.

1.  2. 3. 4.

1. John ____*goes fishing*____ every weekend. 2. Lisa _____ after work.

3. Richard _____ in the park. 4. They_____ every summer.

A Look at the pictures and make sentences using the prompts as in the example.

1.

Lucy / like / play the piano

→ Lucy likes playing the piano.

2.

Kathy / enjoy / listen to music

→ _____

3.

I / put off / do my work

→ _____

4.

they / enjoy / bake and eat cupcakes

→ _____

B Look at the table below and write sentences about Peter using the *-ing* form. Then, complete it for yourself and make sentences about you using the *-ing* form.

	avoid	don't mind	hate	enjoy	can't stand	will stop
ride a bicycle				√		
wake up early					√	
brush his teeth			√			
fight with his sister	√					
clean his room		√				
play computer games						√

1. Peter enjoys riding a bicycle.   I _____.

2. _____   I _____.

3. _____   I _____.

4. _____   I _____.

5. _____   I _____.

6. _____   I _____.

C Use the given words to make sentences with gerunds and infinitives.

1. I hate / do my homework

   I hate doing my homework.

   I hate to do my homework.

2. it / began / rain

3. he/ love / go to soccer games

4. Nancy / hate / drive on city streets / during rush hour

D Complete the sentences with a form of *go* and the given words.

1. I love to swim. Last night, my dad and I swam for hours.

   → Last night, my dad and I ___*went swimming*___. (swim)

2. I love to put up a small tent by a stream, make a fire, and listen to the sounds of the forest during the night.

   → I love to _____. (camp)

3. Yesterday, Karen visited a department store and bought some clothes.

   → Yesterday, Karen _____. (shop)

4. Every morning Chris runs through the park.

   → Every morning Chris _____. (jog)

E Make sentences to describe the pictures as in the example.

1.

   climb rocks / dangerous

   Climbing rocks is dangerous.

2.

   jog every day / good for your health

3.

   speak in English / hard at first

4.

   sleep well / essential for health

A Look at the example and practice with a partner. Use the words below or invent your own. (Then change roles and practice again.)

 In my free time, I enjoy listening to music. How about you?

 I like traveling around the country.

1.

listen to music
→ travel around the country

2.

go to a play
→ learn about different cultures

3.

watch movies
→ ride a bicycle

4.

read beautiful poems
→ take pictures of people on the street

5.

watch a sitcom
→ jog in the park

6.

walk along the beach
→ draw pictures

B Work with a partner. Read about Diana and complete the table below about you. Ask and answer questions as in the example.

DIANA | YOU

LIKE: meet new people
DISLIKE: stay at home
WANT TO BE: an anchorwoman
WOULD LIKE: travel all over the world
HOPE: be rich and successful

What does Diana like doing?

She likes meeting new people.

What do you like doing?

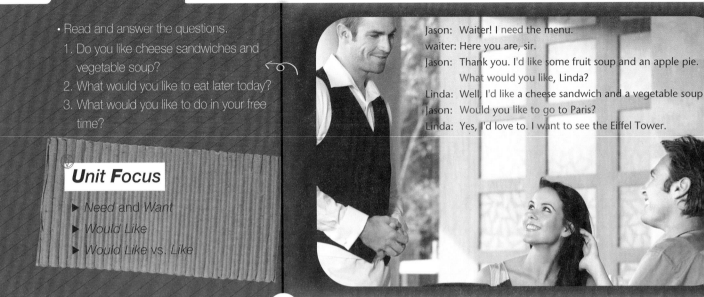

Unit 19 — Need & Want / Would Like

• Read and answer the questions.
1. Do you like cheese sandwiches and vegetable soup?
2. What would you like to eat later today?
3. What would you like to do in your free time?

Jason: Waiter! I need the menu.
waiter: Here you are, sir.
Jason: Thank you. I'd like some fruit soup and an apple pie. What would you like, Linda?
Linda: Well, I'd like a cheese sandwich and a vegetable soup.
Jason: Would you like to go to Paris?
Linda: Yes, I'd love to. I want to see the Eiffel Tower.

Unit Focus

▶ Need and Want
▶ Would Like
▶ Would Like vs. Like

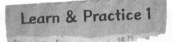

Need and Want

- *Need* is stronger than *want*. *Need* gives the idea that something is very important. *Want* is something you would like to have. It is not absolutely necessary, but it would be a good thing to have.

- *Need* and *want* are followed by a noun or by an infinitive (*to* + base verb). We use *need* + an infinitive to talk about things we think are necessary to do.

I **need** food.   We **want** some cookies.

I **need to** go to the dentist.   She **wants to** drink some milk.

Verb	Object
need	a noun *or* an infinitive
want	

A Write *to* where necessary. Put X where no word is necessary.

1. I want __X__ some oranges.

2. I need __to__ visit my home country.

3. I need _____ a wake-up call in the morning.

4. We want _____ go to the zoo.

5. Do you want _____ some curry and rice?

6. She wants _____ a seat for the rock concert.

7. Susan needs _____ a smartphone.

8. Why do you want _____ be an actor?

Would Like

- We use *would like* and *want* to talk about things we want. The meaning is the same, but *would like* is usually more polite than *want*.
- We use *would like* with a noun or an infinitive (*to* + base verb). In questions, we use *would* before the subject.

I'm thirsty. I **want** a bottle of water.
I'm thirsty. I **would like** a bottle of water.

Affirmative Statements

Subject	*Would Like*	Object
I/You We/They He/She/Tom	would like (= 'd like) / wouldn't like	a noun *or* an infinitive

I'd like to travel around the world.
I wouldn't like to travel around the world.
Q: **Would** you **like to travel** around the world?
A: **Yes, I would. / No, I wouldn't.**

Yes/No Questions

Would	Subject	*Like*	Object	Short Answers	
Would	you/he/she they	like	some water? / to go?	Yes, I/we **would**. he/she **would**. you **would**. they **would**.	No, I/we **wouldn't**. he/she **wouldn't**. you **wouldn't**. they **wouldn't**.

* We rarely use *would like* with *I* or *we* in the interrogative.

A Use the cues to make sentences with *would like* or *would like to*.

1. Sara / go to the zoo → *Sara would like to go to the zoo.*

2. He / a cup of coffee. → _____

3. She / have a cup of green tea → _____

4. Mary / some cheese on her pasta → _____

5. We / make a snowman → _____

6. They / go snowboarding → _____

B Look at the prompts below and write questions using *would like*. Then complete the short answers.

1. she / a bottle of mineral water

Q: Would she like a bottle of mineral water?

A: Yes, she would   .

2. he / learn Japanese

Q: _____

A: No, _____.

3. you / have something to eat

Q: _____

A: Yes, _____.

4. they / some dessert

Q: _____

A: No, _____.

5. Jessica / go to the movie theater

Q: _____

A: Yes, _____.

Learn & Practice 3

Would Like vs. Like

- We use *like* to talk about things you always, usually, or often enjoy.
- We use *would like* to talk about things you want now, or at some time in the future.

I **would like** to go to the amusement park.
(*I would like to go to the amusement park* means I want to go to the amusement park.)

I **like** to go to the amusement park.
(*I like to go to the amusement park* means I enjoy the amusement park.)

A Complete the sentences with *like / not like* + *to*-infinitive or *would like* + *to*-infinitive using the words in brackets.

1. She ___doesn't like to watch___ (watch) TV. She hates it.

2. They _____ (go) to the beach as the weather is very nice today.

3. My friend _____ (study) science because he says it is too difficult for him.

4. _____ you _____ (come) to Anna's party next Monday?

5. _____ your mother _____ (do) the gardening? ~ Yes, very much.

A Rewrite these sentences using *like* or *would like* as in the example.

1. She's crazy about cars.

   → *She likes cars.* _____

2. He plans to go to Egypt for his next trip.

   → _____

3. She loves to dance.

   → _____

4. They want to go to the zoo.

   → _____

5. Bob hopes to become a professional singer one day.

   → _____

6. She enjoys spending her time at home.

   → _____

7. Why do you want to become a movie star?

   → _____

B Read this list and write if you *would like* to do or *wouldn't like* to do these things.

1. learn Chinese

   → *I would/wouldn't like to learn Chinese.*

2. become a K-pop star

   → _____

3. meet a movie star

   → _____

4. have a laptop

   → _____

5. travel around the world

   → _____

6. be very famous

   → _____

7. have a smartphone

   → _____

8. have more homework

   → _____

9. go to Canada on vacation

   → _____

10. go to the movies tonight

    → _____

C Use the prompts to write sentences as in the example. Use an infinitive where necessary.

1. I / want / drink / some water   →   *I want to drink some water.*

2. She / need / a cup of coffee   →   _____

3. He / need / buy a new coat   →   _____

4. I / want / play soccer with you   →   _____

5. I / not need / a new car   →   _____

6. Lisa / want / a salad with her pasta   →   _____

D What do you say to Olivia in these situations? Use *Would you like to...?* and the words in brackets.

1. You want to go to the party tonight. You hope Olivia will go too.
   → You say: *Would you like to go to the party tonight?*   (go)

2. You want to play volleyball tomorrow. You hope Olivia will play with you.
   → You say: _____   (play)

3. You want to go to Korea next week. You hope Olivia will go with you.
   → You say: _____   (go)

4. Olivia wants to write a letter. She doesn't have a pen, but you have one.
   → You say: _____   (borrow)

E Complete the questions for each answer. Use *do you like* or *would you like*.

1. Q: _____*Would you like*_____ a bottle of mineral water? A: Yes, thanks.

2. Q: _____ oranges? A: Yes, I love them.

3. Q: _____ some coffee? A: No, thank you.

4. Q: _____ something to eat? A: No, thanks. I'm not hungry.

5. Q: _____ your new job? A: Yes, I'm enjoying it.

A Look at the example and practice with a partner. Use the words below or invent your own. (Then change roles and practice again.)

1.

 Where would you like to go on a holiday?

 I'd like to go to Korea because I want to see the Seoul Tower.

1.

Korea / the Seoul Tower

2.

Paris / the Eiffel Tower

3.

Egypt / the Pyramids

4.

England / Big Ben

5.

Italy / the Leaning Tower of Pisa

B Work with a partner. Ask and answer questions.

Do you like orange juice?
Would you like a glass of orange juice?

Do you like to play tennis?
Would you like to play tennis with me?

Do you like orange juice?

Yes, I do. / No, I don't.

Yes, please (I would).
/ No, thank you.

Would you like a glass of orange juice?

Do you like to go shopping?
Would you like to go shopping
with me this Saturday?

Do you like pizza?
Would you like some pizza right now?

Do you like to watch TV?
What would you like to watch on
television?

What do you like to do on weekends?
What would you like to do this
weekend?

Do you like ham and cheese sandwiches?
Would you like to have a ham and cheese
sandwich tonight?

• Decide which of the following statements is True and which is False. Write T(for True) or F(for False) in the boxes provided.

Unit Focus

▸ Comparatives
▸ Spelling Rules: Adjectives, Adverbs
▸ As...As and Not As...As

1. **Africa is bigger than Asia.** ☐
2. **The Caribbean Sea is deeper than the Mediterranean Sea.** ☐
3. **The Han River is longer than the Amazon River.** ☐
4. **Mount Everest is higher than Mount Baekdu.** ☐
5. **The USA is larger than Canada.** ☐
6. **Lake Baikal is deeper than the Caspian Sea.** ☐

Learn & Practice 1

Comparatives

- We use the comparative form + *than* to compare two people, animals, or things. An adjective and an adverb in the comparative form are usually followed by the word *than*.

Comparative: Adjective + *-er than*	Comparative: Adverb + *-er than*

A basketball is **bigger than** a baseball.	The deer runs fast. The cheetah runs **faster than** the deer.

Ⓐ Look at the pictures and complete the sentences. Use the comparative form of the words in brackets.

1.
(cheap)

The bicycle is ___cheaper___ than the car.

2.
(long)

Sunny's hair is _____ than Tom's hair.

3.
(hard)

Joe plays _____ than any other player in the team.

Spelling Rules: Adjectives

	Adjective	Comparative	Adjective	Comparative
Adjective + **-(e)r**	tall small nice	tall**er** small**er** nic**er**	slow short cheap	slow**er** short**er** cheap**er**
Double Consonant	bi**g** fa**t**	big**ger** fat**ter**	thi**n** ho**t**	thin**ner** hot**ter**
Drop **-y** + **-ier**	eas**y** prett**y**	eas**ier** prett**ier**	heav**y** happ**y**	heav**ier** happ**ier**
For most 2 or more syllable adjectives, **more** is used.	famous interesting	**more** famous **more** interesting	expensive difficult	**more** expensive **more** difficult

Spelling Rules: Adverbs

	Adverb	Comparative	Adverb	Comparative
More is used with adverbs that end in **-ly**.	slowly loudly	**more** slowly **more** loudly	quickly beautifully	**more** quickly **more** beautifully
Adverb + **-(e)r**	fast late	fast**er** lat**er**	hard	hard**er**

＊Exception: earl**y** → earl**ier**

A Write the comparative form of each word.

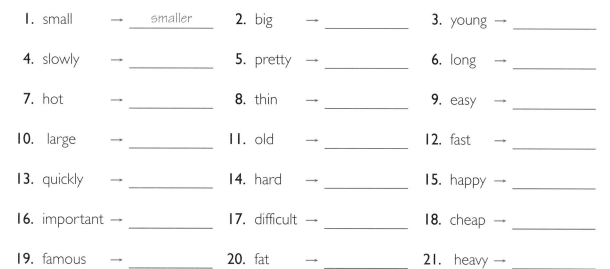

1. small → _smaller_ 2. big → _____ 3. young → _____

4. slowly → _____ 5. pretty → _____ 6. long → _____

7. hot → _____ 8. thin → _____ 9. easy → _____

10. large → _____ 11. old → _____ 12. fast → _____

13. quickly → _____ 14. hard → _____ 15. happy → _____

16. important → _____ 17. difficult → _____ 18. cheap → _____

19. famous → _____ 20. fat → _____ 21. heavy → _____

As...As and Not As...As

- We use *as...as* to show that two things or people are the similar/same in some way.

- We use *not as...as* to show that two things or people are different in some way.

Olivia and Jane are twins.

Olivia is **as** *tall* **as** Jane.

(= Olivia and Jane are the same height.)

Olivia is **as** *old* **as** Jane.

(= Olivia and Jane are the same age.)

My grandfather is 77 years old.

My grandmother is 72 years old.

She is **not as** *old* **as** him.

= She is young**er than** him.

= He is old**er than** her.

A Complete the sentences with *as...as* and the adjectives in brackets.

1. My mother is _____ *as old as* _____ (old) my father.

2. Brian is _____ (tall) his sister.

3. Joe's car isn't _____ (clean) Mark's car.

4. The weather in Japan isn't _____ (cold) that in Korea.

5. A tiger is _____ (dangerous) an alligator.

6. Her room is _____ (big) my house.

B Change the sentences as in the example. Use *not as...as*.

1. Sunny is prettier than her sister. → *Sunny's sister isn't as pretty as Sunny.*

2. You are older than me. → _____

3. John is taller than Bob. → _____

4. She studies harder than me. → _____

Super Writing

A Look at the pictures. Make full sentences using a comparative form.

1.

Steve / Lisa (tall)

Steve is taller than Lisa.

2.

Daniel's hair / Jessica's hair (long)

_____

3.

the smartphone / the MP3 player (expensive)

_____

4.

the rugby ball / the tennis ball (big)

_____

5.

the car / the bicycle (heavy)

_____

6.

Susan / her husband (thin)

_____

B Rewrite or join the following sentences using *as...as*.

1. The papaya is sweet. The mango is sweet, too.
   → *The papaya is as sweet as the mango.*

2. My dog is fierce. Your dog is fierce, too.
   → _____

3. Both the white dress and the blue dress are expensive.
   → _____

4. Both Jessica and her sister are artistic.
   → _____

5. Mark and Linda are both of the same age.
   → _____

C Read the questions and answer them as in the example.

1.

Canada **vs.** China
(big)   (small)

Q: Which country is bigger, Canada or China?
A: *Canada is bigger than China.*

Q: Which country is smaller, Canada or China?
A: *China is smaller than Canada.*

2.

the Nile **vs.** the Han River
(long)   (short)

Q: Which river is longer, the Nile or the Han River?
A: _____

Q: Which river is shorter, the Nile or the Han river?
A: _____

3.

English **vs.** Korean
(easy)   (difficult)

Q: Which one is easier, English or Korean?
A: _____

Q: Which one is more difficult, English or Korean?
A: _____

D Rewrite each sentence with *not as...as*, but keep the same meaning.

1. Paris is more beautiful than London.   →   *London is not as beautiful as Paris.*

2. Geroge is heavier than Nick.   →   _____

3. The sun is bigger than the earth.   →   _____

4. William speaks more slowly than Peter.   →   _____

E Read and complete the sentences as in the example.

1. Nancy can't speak fast, but Lisa can.   →   Nancy can't speak ____*as fast as Lisa*____ .

2. Eric runs fast, but Kathy doesn't.   →   Eric runs _____ .

3. Amy drives carelessly, but Scott doesn't.   →   Amy drives _____ .

4. Bob doesn't work hard, but Alice does.   →   Bob doesn't work _____ .

5. Liz pronounced each word clearly, but Susan didn't.   →   Liz pronounced each word _____ _____ .

A Look at the example and practice with a partner. Use the words below or invent your own. (Then change roles and practice again.)

1.

Sally / funny

I.

Are you as funny as Sally?

No, I'm not as funny as Sally. She is funnier than me.

2.

Bob / outgoing

3.

Jennifer / energetic

4.

Karen / studious

5.

Eric / serious

B Work with a partner. Look at the activities in the pictures below and compare them using the words in the box.

watching TV   reading   swimming   cleaning the house   riding a bike   drawing

cooking a meal   listening to music   exercising   doing the laundry   washing the dishes

I think that reading is more interesting than watching TV. What do you think?

I think that...

interesting	exciting	boring
easy	difficult	happy
fun	hard	safe

A Use the prompts to make sentences as in the example.

1. Eric likes planes. He / a pilot → *Eric likes planes. He wants to be a pilot.*

2. Sunny likes animals. She / a vet →

3. Jane likes movies. She / an actress →

4. They like soccer. They / soccer players →

B Use the prompts below to make sentences as in the example.

1. an ostrich / a penguin (big) → *An ostrich is bigger than a penguin.*

2. gold / silver (expensive) →

3. feathers / stones (light) →

4. a car / a bicycle (fast) →

C Complete the sentences with to or for.

1. Kelly called the station ___*to*___ ask about the London trains.

2. Kelly called the station _____ information about the London trains.

3. We don't need much money _____ buy tickets.

4. We don't need much money _____ tickets.

D Look at the pictures and prompts. Read the questions and answer them.

1.
go to school

Q: What do they need to do?
A: *They need to go to school.*

2.
a wake-up call in the morning

Q: What does he need?
A:

3.
relax for a while

Q: What do you need to do?
A:

E Rewrite each sentence with not as...as, but keep the same meaning.

1. Seoul is more beautiful than Tokyo. → *Tokyo is not as beautiful as Seoul.*

2. Kevin is heavier than Lisa. →

3. The earth is bigger than the moon. →

4. Steve drives more slowly than Amy. →

F **Match column A with column B to make correct sentences.**

A	B
1. Writing letters to friends	a. is very tiring.
2. The baby started	b. is bad for your teeth.
3. Running long distances	c. crying when I left the room.
4. They went	d. skiing last winter.
5. Eating lots of sugar	e. is one of my hobbies.
6. Tom doesn't like	f. washing the dishes.

G **Complete the questions with _would you like_ or _do you like_.**

1. Q: ___Would you like___ some oranges? A: No, thanks.

2. Q: What _____ to have for dinner tonight? A: A bowl of tomato soup, please.

3. Q: What kind of music _____? A: I prefer K-pop music.

4. Q: _____ to watch scary movies? A: No, I don't. I prefer romantic comedies.

H **Look at the pictures and complete the sentences. Use _go/goes_ + _-ing_.**

1.  2.  3.  4.

1. Tomorrow, we'll ___go swimming___ .

2. Do you _____ every winter?

3. My mom enjoys _____ .

4. They _____ every weekend.

I **Look and answer the questions below, as in the example.**

1.

visit her grandparents

2.

buy some books

3.

reserve a flight

Q: Why did Anna go to Chicago?

A: _She went to Chicago to_

visit her grandparents.

Q: Why did Olivia go to the bookstore?

A: _____

_____

Q: Why did they go to the travel agency?

A: _____

_____

You are my
Grammar &
Speaking

2 Student Book

Answer Key

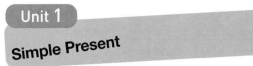

Answer Key

Unit 1
Simple Present
p. 8

Learn & Practice 1
A **1.** has **2.** doesn't like **3.** needs **4.** don't want

Learn & Practice 2
A **1.** lives **2.** speaks **3.** pushes **4.** cries **5.** stays **6.** buys
 7. makes **8.** does **9.** has

B **1.** wears **2.** gets up **3.** goes **4.** reads **5.** hurries
 6. plays

Learn & Practice 3
A **1.** Q: Does he have a smartphone? A: he does
 2. Q: Does she know his family? A: she doesn't
 3. Q: Do they need more money? A: they do

Learn & Practice 4
A **1.** comes (Fact) **2.** arrives (Future) **3.** begin (Future)
 4. doesn't (Habit)

Super Writing
A **1.** Q: Does Bob work at a restaurant?
 A: No, he doesn't.
 2. Q: Does Ava exercise every morning?
 A: No, she doesn't.
 3. Q: Does Jane's taxi go to the subway station?
 A: No, it doesn't.
 4. Q: Does Tom always study at home in the evening?
 A: No, he doesn't.
 5. Q: Does the bus come every ten minutes?
 A: No, it doesn't.

B **1.** doesn't watch TV. She studies Korean every day.
 2. doesn't teach French. She teaches English.
 3. doesn't have a cat. She has a puppy.
 4. doesn't play basketball on Tuesday afternoons. He
 plays tennis on Tuesday afternoons.

C **1.** begins at 2:00 tomorrow
 2. leaves at 7:00 tonight
 3. does the laundry shop open tomorrow
 4. leaves at 6:00 p.m. tomorrow

D **1.** Q: Does Chris watch a DVD in the evenings?
 A: No, he doesn't. He listens to music.
 2. Q: Does Lisa play on the computer in the evenings?

A: No, she doesn't. She reads books.
 3. Q: Does Rachel take exercise in the evenings?
 A: No, she doesn't. She has an English lesson.
 4. Q: Does John ride a bicycle in the evenings?
 A: No, he doesn't. He rides a skateboard.

Unit 2
Present Progressive
p. 14

Learn & Practice 1
A **1.** is making (Right Now)
 2. am taking (Around Now)
 3. is studying (Around Now)
 4. is snowing (Right Now)
 5. are listening (Right Now)

Learn & Practice 2
A **1.** are looking **2.** is enjoying **3.** am sitting **4.** is eating
 5. is studying **6.** are wearing

Learn & Practice 3
A **1.** Q: Is Jessica cooking chicken? A: Yes, she is.
 2. Q: Is the girl wearing a hat? A: No, she isn't.
 3. Q: Is peter playing a computer game? A: Yes, he is.
 4. Q: Are you writing a letter? A: No, I'm not.
 5. Q: Is the dog sitting on the chair? A: Yes, it is.
 6. Q: Are they celebrating their anniversary?
 A: No, they aren't.

Super Writing
A **1.** Q: Is he painting the car?
 A: No, he isn't. He is painting the wall.
 2. Q: Is she sitting?
 A: No, she isn't. She is walking.
 3. Q: Is the girl reading a magazine?
 A: No, she isn't. She is reading a book.
 4. Q: Are they watching TV?
 A: No, they aren't. They are seeing a movie.

B **1.** Is she riding a bicycle?
 She isn't riding a bicycle.
 2. Is he watching a horror movie?
 He isn't watching a horror movie.
 3. Are you talking on your mobile phone?

You aren't talking on your mobile phone.

  4. Are you/we playing basketball?

    We/You aren't playing basketball.

  5. Are they wearing suits?

    They aren't wearing suits.

  6. Am I / Are you doing the right exercise?

    I'm not / You aren't doing the right exercise.

C **I.** Q: Is the girl wearing pants?

    A: Yes, she is.

  2. Q: Is the mother wearing a white dress?

    A: No, she isn't.

  3. Q: Are the mother and father holding hands?

    A: No, they aren't.

  4. Q: Are the mother and father wearing hats?

    A: No, they aren't.

  5. Q: Are the people standing?

    A: Yes, they are.

  6. Q: Is the father holding his son?

    A: No, he isn't.

D **I.** No, she isn't doing her homework. She is eating an ice cream.

  2. No, he isn't riding a bicycle. He is skateboarding.

  3. No, she isn't windsurfing. She is flying a kite.

Unit 3
Simple Present vs. Present Progressive p. 20

Learn & Practice 1
A **I.** shining **2.** lives **3.** singing **4.** helping **5.** take

  6. sitting

Learn & Practice 2
A **I.** wears (Fact)

  2. listening (Complaint)

  3. complaining (Complaint)

  4. eats (Habit)

Learn & Practice 3
A **I.** is flying (Future Plan)

  2. will drive (Prediction)

  3. is studying (Now)

  4. am seeing (Future Plan)

  5. will go (Prediction)

B **I.** is playing tennis

  2. is working in her office

  3. are going to the concert

Super Writing
A **I.** drinks; is drinking

  2. don't work; am working

  3. walk; are riding

  4. plays; is playing

B **I.** She is cleaning the room.

  2. She watches TV.

  3. She is wearing a scarf.

  4. He drinks orange juice.

C **I.** She is arriving in Seoul at 9:00.

  2. She is meeting Bob and Tom at 10:00.

  3. She is having lunch with Ava between 12:00 and 2:00.

  4. She is waiting for Kevin in the hotel lobby.

  5. She is returning to the hotel and preparing for a meeting on Tuesday at 9:00.

D **I.** are always losing your smartphone

  2. is always breaking down

  3. am always making the same mistake

  4. are always forgetting your books

Unit 4
p. 26
The Verb Be

Learn & Practice 1
A **I.** were **2.** was **3.** am **4.** is **5.** are **6.** were

Learn & Practice 2
A **I.** We aren't young.

  2. She wasn't late for school.

  3. They weren't in the park.

  4. He isn't at the library today.

  5. He wasn't a musician.

Learn & Practice 3
A **I.** Q: Is Tom a nurse? A: he isn't

  2. Q: Were they teachers? A: they were

  3. Q: Is Angelina Joli American? A: she is

  4. Q: Is Cindy at home? A: she isn't

5. Q: Was he in the museum? A: he wasn't

6. Q: Were the girls late for school? A: they were

Super Writing

A 1. are Japanese cities

2. is an American businessman

3. is the capital of Korea

4. are my favorite subjects

5. is very good at the Chinese martial art, kung fu

6. was a painter

7. were famous painters

B 1. Q: was Ava last night

A: She was at the movie theater.

2. Q: was Susan yesterday afternoon

A: She was at the airport.

3. Q: are Bob and Jane now

A: They are at a restaurant.

4. Q: are they now

A: They are at the shopping center.

C 1. Q: Is Tom here today?

A: No, he isn't.

2. Q: Was Nancy busy yesterday?

A: No, she wasn't.

3. Q: Is Steve a basketball player?

A: No, he isn't.

4. Q: Were Sunny and Isabel bakers 10 years ago?

A: No, they weren't.

5. Q: Are your sisters elementary school students?

A: No, they aren't.

6. Q: Was Kelly at home yesterday?

A: No, she wasn't.

D 1. Q: Are they oranges?

A: No, they aren't. They are lemons.

2. Q: Is Jessica a student?

A: No, she isn't. She is a teacher.

3. Q: Are they at the bus stop?

A: No, they aren't. They are at the train station.

4. Q: Were you in Korea last year?

A: No, I wasn't. I was in Egypt. /

No, we weren't. We were in Egypt.

Review Test (Unit 1-4)
p. 32

A 1. walks; is riding 2. watch; are having

3. drink; am drinking 4. is visiting; visits

B 1. drives; fights; is putting; is wearing

C 1. He is going to the movie theater with Bob on Wednesday.

2. He is playing tennis with his sister on Monday.

3. He is going to the doctor at 1:30 on Thursday.

4. He is flying to New York on Friday.

5. He is meeting Isabel on Tuesday.

D 1. I was at home yesterday.

2. Jane and Tom were tired yesterday.

3. It was a sunny day yesterday.

4. We weren't at work yesterday.

5. You weren't at school yesterday.

E 1. Does your brother drive fast?

2. Does Peter play the guitar every day?

3. Do Ava and Cindy go shopping on Mondays?

4. Do the children watch TV in the afternoon?

F 1. Q: Is she playing soccer?

A: No, she isn't. She is playing tennis.

2. Q: Is he driving to work?

A: No, he isn't. He is reading a newspaper.

3. Q: Are they watching TV?

A: No, they aren't. They are washing the/a car.

Unit 5
p. 34

Simple Past 1

Learn & Practice 1

A 1. rained 2. didn't wait 3. opened 4. didn't work

5. stayed 6. didn't watch

Learn & Practice 2

A 1. Q: Did she practice the piano? A: she didn't

2. Q: Did he enjoy his vacation? A: he did

3. Q: Did they like the movie? A: they didn't

4. Q: Did it rain all day? A: it did

5. Q: Did you watch the discussion? A: I didn't

B 1. did he enjoy the music?

2. did she remember it?

3. did you like the movie?

4. did you give them any money?

Learn & Practice 3

A 1. didn't use to watch 2. used to drink 3. used to live

4. didn't use to like 5. used to play

Super Writing

A 1. Q: Did Tom play basketball yesterday?

   A: No, he didn't. He painted a picture.

   2. Q: Did Olivia go to the movie last night?

   A: No, she didn't. She listened to music.

   3. Q: Did it rain here last month?

   A: No, it didn't. It snowed here.

   4. Q: Did Sunny watch a DVD last night?

   A: No, she didn't. She talked to John on the phone.

B Five years ago, Jason <u>was a student at the City College</u> <u>of San Francisco. He wanted to be a science teacher,</u> <u>and he needed to take many science classes. He liked</u> <u>his classes. In his free time, he played volleyball with his</u> <u>friends. His family was in Korea, and he sometimes</u> <u>visited them.</u>

D 1. The Inuit used to travel by dogsled. Now, they don't anymore. They travel by snowmobile.

   2. The Inuit used to get light from oil lamps. Now, they don't anymore. They have electric light bulbs.

   3. The Inuit used to travel by kayak. Now, they don't anymore. They travel by floatplane.

   4. The Inuit used to live in igloos and tents. Now, they don't anymore. They live in modern houses.

   5. The Inuit used to hunt caribous with arrows. Now, they don't anymore. They hunt caribous with rifles.

E 1. Children didn't have smartphones.

   2. People didn't watch television.

   3. A lot of women stayed at home.

   4. Children didn't eat hamburgers.

   5. Homes didn't have computers.

   6. Mothers washed clothes by hand.

Unit 6
Simple Past 2
p. 40

Learn & Practice 1

A 1. decided 2. invited 3. started 4. brushed 5. cried

   6. stopped

Learn & Practice 2

A 1. Kathy drank milk.

   2. Peter rode his bicycle.

   3. I studied for the chemistry test.

   4. They made a model plane.

   5. We ate lunch.

6. She went to Africa.

Learn & Practice 3

A 1. <u>After she ate dinner,</u> she went to the movies.

   → She went to the movies after she ate dinner.

   2. He had lunch <u>before he finished his work.</u>

   → Before he finished his work, he had lunch.

   3. She got a good job <u>after she graduated.</u>

   → After she graduated, she got a good job.

   4. <u>After he did the dishes,</u> he watched TV.

   → He watched TV after he did the dishes.

Super Writing

A 1. → Tom didn't go to work on Monday.

   → He went to the movies on Monday.

   2. → Tom didn't do his laundry on Sunday.

   → He studied and watched TV on Sunday.

   3. → Tom didn't go out to dinner on Saturday.

   → He slept late on Saturday.

   4. → Tom didn't buy a pink wallet on Friday.

   → He wrote an email to his friends on Friday.

C 1. → After he brushed his teeth, he went to bed.

   → Before he went to bed, he brushed his teeth.

   2. → After they got married, they had a baby.

   → Before they had a baby, they got married.

   3. → After she succeeded, she helped poor people.

   → Before she helped poor people, she succeeded.

   4. → After he learned to walk, he rode a bicycle.

   → Before he rode a bicycle, he learned to walk.

D 1. Q: Did Olivia eat a sandwich last night?

   A: No, she didn't. She ate a hamburger.

   2. Q: Did Kathy break her ankle two days ago?

   A: No, she didn't. She hurt her knee.

   3. Q: Did Cindy and Mark watch a DVD yesterday?

   A: No, they didn't. They went to the movie theater.

   4. Q: Did the girls walk in the park yesterday?

   A: No, they didn't. They rode their bicycles.

Unit 7
Past Progressive 1
p. 46

Learn & Practice 1

A 1. Jane was running very fast.

   2. My mom was doing the dishes.

   3. He was studying hard for the test.

143

4. Sunny and Jessica were riding a roller coaster.

Learn & Practice 2

A 1. wasn't reading; was listening

  2. weren't preparing; were riding

  3. weren't taking; were walking

  4. wasn't brushing; was washing

Learn & Practice 3

1. Q: Was she smiling at you? A: she was

2. Q: Was he writing a composition? A: he wasn't

3. Q: Was it raining last night? A: it was

4. Q: Were they studying Korean? A: they weren't

5. Q: Was Jane talking with Tom? A: she was

6. Q: Was William washing his car? A: he wasn't

7. Q: Were the women sitting in a cafe? A: they were

Super Writing

A 1. was sitting at her desk

  2. were seeing a scary movie

  3. was washing the dishes

  4. were having dinner

  5. was talking on the phone

  6. was playing the drums

B 1. No, she wasn't having dinner. She was watching TV.

  2. No, they weren't reading books. They were sleeping on the bed.

  3. No, he wasn't listening to the news. He was working very hard.

  4. No, they weren't jogging in the park. They were taking pictures.

C 1. Q: Was she driving the car?

    A: No, she wasn't. She was jogging.

  2. Q: Was the boy swimming in the pool?

    A: No, he wasn't. He was flying his kite.

  3. Q: Was Kathy watering the plants?

    A: No, he wasn't. She was taking the subway.

D 1. Q: What were you doing at 7:00?

    A: I was taking a shower.

  2. Q: What were you doing at 9:00?

    A: I was walking in the park.

  3. Q: What were you doing at 12:00?

    A: I was eating lunch in the restaurant.

  4. Q: What were you doing at 7:30?

    A: I was doing the laundry.

Unit 8
Past Progressive 2

p. 52

Learn & Practice 1

A 1. Where were you living

  2. Why was Sunny driving

  3. Where were they going

  4. What was Jane doing

Learn & Practice 2

A 1. was driving 2. was running 3. was watching

  4. was studying 5. Were; driving 6. were walking

B 1. was having 2. was going 3. was ironing

  4. were singing and dancing

C 1. was studying; saw

  2. was washing; got

  3. came; was eating

  4. was brushing; arrived

  5. was sleeping; rang

  6. was waiting; began

Super Writing

A 1. A: No, he wasn't eating a hamburger.

    A: He was playing volleyball.

  2. A: No, he wasn't surfing the net.

    A: He was washing a/the/his dog.

  3. A: No, she wasn't washing the dishes.

    A: She was watching TV.

  4. A: No, she wasn't cleaning the house.

    A: She was eating a sandwich.

  5. A: They were reading newspapers.

  6. A: They were studying.

  7. A: No, he wasn't speaking on the phone.

    A: He was cleaning the house.

  8. A: They were drinking (some) milk.

  9. A: No, they weren't. They were playing soccer.

  10. A: She was painting the table.

B 1. Jeff was eating a hamburger when the email arrived.

  2. While Kathy was driving to the bank, the cell phone rang.

  3. William was running in the street when it started raining.

  4. Bill was watching a scary movie when his friend arrived.

C 1. Q: What was Sarah doing when you called her yesterday?

A: She was swimming when I called her yesterday.

2. Q: What was Ava doing when you came home yesterday?

A: She was reading a novel when I came home yesterday.

3. Q: What was your mother doing when you came home from school?

A: She was doing the laundry when I came home from school.

p. 58

Review Test (Unit 5-8)

A 1. began; was riding

2. was driving; crashed

3. was watching; rang

4. corrected; were working

B 1. Lisa used to play tennis in her childhood.

2. Kevin used to eat a lot of pizza in his childhood.

C 1. Nancy was sleeping when the cell phone rang.

2. While Alice was driving, a man crossed the street.

3. They were walking in the park when it started raining.

4. My dad was brushing his teeth when I arrived at home.

D 1. Yesterday I was tired during the day.

2. You were sick last week.

3. You had a cough and a fever.

4. She had a bad headache.

5. This morning Kevin was nervous.

E 1. broke 2. drove 3. woke 4. went 5. came

6. ate 7. did 8. took

F 1. → Before we arrived at the airport, the plane landed.

→ After the plane landed, we arrived at the airport.

2. → Before I went to a movie. I finished my homework.

→ After I finished my homework. I went to a movie.

3. → Before they watched TV, they got home from school.

→ After they got home from school, they watched TV.

G 1. Q: What was she doing?

A: She was waiting for a train.

2. Q: What was Dad doing?

A: He was washing the dishes.

3. Q: What were they doing?

A: They were having lunch.

p. 60

Unit 9
The Future Tense 1

Learn & Practice 1

A 1. is going to paint

→ Is Kevin going to paint the house tomorrow? (Prior Plan)

2. is going to rain

→ Is it going to rain? (Future Prediction)

3. are going to watch

→ Are you going to watch TV tonight? (Prior Plan)

4. are going to buy

→ Are they going to buy a new car next month? (Prior Plan)

Learn & Practice 2

A 1. → He won't go to the library.

→ Q: Will he go to the library? A: he won't

2. → They won't eat oranges.

→ Q: Will they eat oranges? A: they will

3. → She won't buy new clothes.

→ Q: Will she buy new clothes? A: she won't

4. → It won't rain tomorrow.

→ Q: Will it rain tomorrow? A: it will

Learn & Practice 3

A 1. are going to get 2. will open 3. will bring

4. are going to go

Super Writing

A 1. She's going to miss the plane.

2. I'm going to buy some fruit.

3. Kevin is going to fall into the river.

4. It's going to rain.

B 1. Q: Will you be at the library tomorrow night?

A: I will

2. Q: Will people live in space colonies?

A: they will

3. Q: Will the train be on time?

A: it won't

4. Q: Will Hunter and Sunny be at the party?

A: they won't

    5. Q: Will Ava arrive in Hong Kong next week?

      A: she will

    6. Q: Will we/you travel around the world in an hour by space shuttle?

      A: we will

C 1. On Monday, she's going to have lunch with John.
She isn't going to go to the movie theater.

    2. On Tuesday, she's going to attend a meeting from 8:00 to 10:00.
She isn't going to have brunch with Tom.

    3. On Wednesday, she's going to go to a computer conference on 58th street.
She isn't going to take a yoga class.

    4. On Thursday, she's going to give a presentation to her boss at 12:00

    5. On Friday, she's going to take the train to Boston.

    6. On Saturday, she's going to meet Lisa outside the movie theater at 7:00.
She isn't going to eat dinner in a restaurant.

D 1. Q: Is Linda going to take the dog for a walk tomorrow?

      A: No, she isn't. She's going to go shopping.

    2. Q: Is Aiden going to take a bus to work tomorrow morning?

      A: No, he isn't. He's going to ride his bicycle to work.

    3. Q: Are the children going to watch a DVD next Wednesday?

      A: No, they aren't. They're going to study math.

Unit 10
The Future Tense 2
p. 66

Learn & Practice 1
A 1. is flying 2. is going to rain 3. begins

Learn & Practice 2
A 1. get; will go 2. say; will give 3. call; will ask
    4. finishes; will go 5. goes; will wear

Learn & Practice 3
A 1. go 2. will go 3. will be 4. throw

Super Writing

A 1. No, he's playing volleyball on Sunday morning.

    2. No, he's seeing John Parker on Monday afternoon.

    3. No, he's cleaning his bedroom on Tuesday evening.

    4. No, he's going to the theater on Thursday night.

    5. No, he's visiting Madame Tussauds museum on Friday afternoon.

    6. No, he's leaving for Mexico on Saturday morning.

B 1. If Shawn runs very fast, he will win the race. / If Shawn doesn't run very fast, he won't win the race.

    2. If you don't take the subway, you'll be late for work. / If you take the subway, you won't be late for work.

    3. If the purse is expensive, Olivia won't buy it. / If the purse isn't expensive, Olivia will buy it.

    4. If you write on the deck, you'll be in trouble. / If you don't write on the desk, you won't be in trouble.

C 1. When I go shopping tomorrow, I will buy a new coat.

    2. After Isabella finishes her homework this evening, she will take a walk.

    3. After Karen does her homework, she's going to go home later in the evening.

    4. Before I go home, I'm going to buy a scarf at the store.

    5. When I see William tomorrow, I will ask him join us for dinner this weekend.

D 1. If you go out without a jacket at night, you'll get a cold.

    2. If you don't eat breakfast, you will be hungry.

    3. If you eat too many chocolates, you will get fat.

    4. If you go to bed early, you won't be tired the next day.

    5. If you lie in the sun, you will get sunburned.

Unit 11
Nouns and Articles
p. 72

Learn & Practice 1
A 1. dishes 2. countries 3. potatoes 4. tomatoes
    5. boxes 6. thieves 7. feet 8. fish 9. women
    10. stories 11. benches 12. leaves

Learn & Practice 2
A 1. N 2. C 3. N 4. C 5. N 6. N 7. C 8. C 9. C
    10. N 11. N 12. C

B 1. book 2. pencils 3. sheep 4. cheese 5. water
  6. puppies

Learn & Practice 3
A 1. an; The; a 2. a; a; the

Super Writing
A 1. The moon moves slowly round the earth.
  2. The sun is very hot today.
  3. I have two girls. The girls are at school.
  4. I don't have a car or an apartment.
  5. The prince of Wales is visiting our town next week.
  6. You can have an apple or oranges. The apple is nice and sweet.
B 1. Yes, there are five balloons.
  2. Yes, there are two schoolbags.
  3. Yes, there are two women.
  4. Yes, there are three boxes.
C 1. cities 2. geese 3. leaves 4. watches 5. ladies
  6. wolves 7. children
D 1. in Egypt
  2. the piano every day
  3. an umbrella this afternoon
  4. The puppy is really cute

Unit 12
Quantity Words
p. 78

Learn & Practice 1
A 1. a sheet/piece of paper 2. two loaves of bread

Learn & Practice 2
A 1. an; some 2. any 3. some; any 4. a

Learn & Practice 3
A 1. Every 2. All 3. Every 4. All

Learn & Practice 4
A 1. much 2. much 3. How many 4. much
  5. How much 6. many
B 1. a lot of books 2. a lot of accidents
  3. a lot of fun things 4. a lot of traffic

Super Writing
A 1. There are some strawberries in the fridge, but there aren't any apples.
  2. There is some milk in the fridge, but there isn't any yogurt.
  3. There are some tomatoes on the table, but there aren't any potatoes.
  4. There is some ice cream in the fridge, but there isn't any chocolate.
  5. There are some oranges in the bag, but there aren't any carrots.
B 1. Every waiter speaks excellent Korean.
  2. Every cook wears uniform.
  3. Every child likes to play.
  4. Every dish comes with a salad.
  5. Every room has a balcony.
  6. Every room has a bathroom.
  7. Every tourist has a travel guide.
  8. Every meal includes dessert.
C 1. She drinks a glass of milk. She doesn't drink any coffee.
  2. Q: How much bread is there?
    A: There are two loaves/pieces/slices of bread.
  3. How many teaspoons of sugar do you take in your tea?
  4. I ate three pieces of cake yesterday.
  5. Q: How much orange juice is there?
    A: There are three bottles/glasses/cups of orange juice.
D 1. I don't have much money.
  2. There are many signs on the road.
  3. I don't put much sugar in my tea.
  4. Do you have many friends?
  5. Seoul has many skyscrapers.
  6. I want to visit many cities in Korea.
  7. Did they ask you many questions?
  8. Does Jane usually buy much fruit?
  9. Tiffany doesn't drink much coffee.

Review Test (Unit 9–12)
p. 84

A 1. a (count) 2. some (noncount) 3. an (count)
  4. some (noncount) 5. some (noncount) 6. a (count)
B 1. two cups of coffee
  2. two loaves of bread
  3. four pieces of cheese
  4. a carton of milk

5. a sheet/piece of paper

6. three bottles of water

C **1.** is going to make

   2. is going to study

   3. are going to graduate

   4. are going to become

   5. is not going to return

D **1.** many → much **2.** any → some **3.** some → any

   4. many → much **5.** much → many

E **1.** Every room has a balcony.

   2. Every student worked hard.

   3. Every student speaks excellent Korean.

   4. Every tourist has a travel guide.

F **1.** Q: What time is he arriving in Seoul?

     A: He's arriving in Seoul at 8:00.

   2. Q: Who is he meeting at 9:00?

     A: He's meeting Susan at the office.

   3. Q: What is he doing between 12:00 and 2:00.

     A: He's having lunch with his boss.

G **1.** is; will get **2.** graduates; will get **3.** asks; will answer

   4. will have; goes

H **1.** much **2.** many **3.** much **4.** many **5.** much

   6. many

5. on July 21, 1969

B **1.** Jane finished high school in 2005.

   2. We have class from ten to eleven.

   3. The family restaurant closes at 10:00 p.m.

   4. I'll wait for Susan until 7 o'clock.

   5. I always feel tired in the morning.

   6. My husband and I fell asleep during the movie.

C **1.** The plane leaves in two hours.

   2. The train leaves in five minutes.

   3. I'll call you in three days.

   4. Jason will be here in four hours.

D **1.** It opens at 8:00 a.m.

   2. She leaves home at 9 o'clock.

   3. It (New Year's Day) is on January 1st.

   4. It (Valentine's Day) is on February 14th.

   5. He goes on vacation in winter.

E **1.** Katie lived in Korea for three years.

     She lived in Korea until 2005.

   2. Cindy lived in Canada for five years.

     She lived in Canada until 2011.

   3. Wilson lived in China for nine years.

     He lived in China until 2008.

Unit 13
Prepositions of Time
p. 86

Learn & Practice 1

A **1.** in **2.** in **3.** at **4.** at **5.** in **6.** in **7.** on **8.** on **9.** in **10.** on

B **1.** at **2.** on **3.** in **4.** on **5.** in **6.** at

C **1.** does Bob go; on **2.** don't play; on

   3. Do you often hang; in **4.** does Carly have; on

Learn & Practice 2

A **1.** before **2.** before **3.** from **4.** until **5.** After **6.** after

B **1.** during **2.** for **3.** during **4.** for **5.** for **6.** during

   7. for **8.** during

Super Writing

A **1.** in the 15th century

   2. on April 11th

   3. at night

   4. at 10 o'clock

Unit 14
Prepositions of Place and Movement
p. 92

Learn & Practice 1

A **1.** next to / by **2.** on **3.** in front of / near **4.** between

   5. at **6.** above

Learn & Practice 2

A **1.** over; along; across **2.** into; out of **3.** up; down

   4. through; from; to

B **1.** into **2.** up **3.** across **4.** around **5.** from **6.** out of

   7. down **8.** through **9.** along

Super Writing

A **1.** On the balcony.

   2. At the bus stop.

   3. At the airport.

   4. On the wall.

   5. In the bus.

   6. On the table.

B **1.** the bank **2.** the record shop **3.** the shoe store

   4. The restaurant **5.** the bookstore

6. the KFC; the bookstore

C 1. through **2.** across **3.** along **4.** from **5.** onto

D 1. No, it isn't. It is opposite the travel agency.

    2. No, it isn't. It is behind the flower shop.

    3. No, it isn't. It is between the movie theater and the shoe store.

    4. No, it isn't. It is across from the museum.

Unit 15

Helping Verbs 1
p. 98

Learn & Practice 1

A 1. could **2.** can **3.** couldn't

B 1. Can you write with your left hand?

    2. Can Jane eat with chopsticks?

    3. Could you speak English when you were younger?

Learn & Practice 2

A 1. shouldn't **2.** should; should

Learn & Practice 3

A 1. have to run

    2. has to wear

    3. must clean

    4. Do we have to work

    5. mustn't (= must not) go out

Super Writing

A 1. You must not talk in the library.

    2. I must study hard for this exam.

    3. Children must drink lots of milk.

    4. You must not stay in the sun for a long time.

    5. They must be here at 9 o'clock.

    6. Students must not leave school early without permission.

B 1. Q: Does Sunny have to work in the afternoon?

    A: No, she doesn't. She has to work in the morning.

    2. Q: Does Mary have to study history tonight?

    A: No, she doesn't. She has to study geography.

    3. Q: Do they have to wash the car every day?

    A: No, they don't. They have to wash the car on the weekend.

    4. Q: Does Jessica have to go to the doctor today?

    A: No, she doesn't. She has to go to the doctor tomorrow.

C 1. Lisa can drive a car now. When she was younger, she could only ride a bicycle.

    2. Jack can play golf now. When he was younger, he could only play soccer.

    3. Wilson can ride a snowboard now. When he was younger, he could only ride a skateboard.

E 1. → She should do exercise more.

    → She shouldn't eat candies.

    2. → She should take a break.

    → She shouldn't work so hard.

    3. → He should use an alarm clock.

    → He shouldn't go to bed late at night.

Unit 16

Helping Verbs 2
p. 104

Learn & Practice 1

A 1. possibility **2.** ability **3.** permission

Learn & Practice 2

A 1. Can I **2.** May I **3.** Could I

Learn & Practice 3

A 1. Can you open the window?

    2. Would/Could you open the door?

    3. Can you turn down the volume?

    4. Would/Could you get me a glass of cold water?

    5. Would/Could you tell me the time?

    6. Can you watch my children for a minute?

Learn & Practice 4

A 1. must be **2.** must not have **3.** must not be

    4. must be **5.** must be **6.** must not be **7.** must like

Super Writing

A 1. → Can I have a drink?

    → Could I have a drink?

    2. → Can you open the door?

    → Could you open the door?

    3. → Can you answer the phone?

    → Could you answer the phone?

    4. → Can I turn on the television?

    → Could I turn on the television?

    5. → Can you help me with my suitcase?

    → Could you help me with my suitcase?

6. → Can I borrow this book?

→ Could I borrow this book?

B 1. may/might/could sell his new car

2. may/might/could become an astronaut

3. may/might/could become famous

4. may/might/could win the race

5. may/might/could visit him tomorrow

6. may/might/could be at the library

C 1. He must not be at home.

2. She must be happy.

3. She must not be American.

4. She must be rich.

5. It must be for you.

6. They must be in the kitchen.

7. He must not have many friends.

E 1. Can I go to a party tonight?

2. Can I invite some friends to dinner?

3. May I see your ticket?

4. Could you open the door?

5. Could you teach me how to drive a car?

Review Test (Unit 13–16)

p. 110

A 1. c 2. b 3. c 4. b 5. c 6. a

B 1. Can I borrow your camera?

2. May I use the phone?

3. Can I borrow your dictionary?

4. May I have a cup of coffee?

C 1. He read the newspaper from 7:00 to 8:00.

2. He washed his car from 9:00 to 10:00.

3. He played tennis from 11:00 to 12:00.

4. He talked to his friends from 12:00 to 1:00.

D 1. You should eat

2. You shouldn't eat

3. You should take

4. You shouldn't smoke

5. You shouldn't drink

E 1. You must take it to the vet.

2. She must take an aspirin.

3. You must not drink it.

4. You must not swim here.

F 1. in 2. on 3. in 4. at

G 1. Would/Could you open the window?

2. Would/Could you answer the phone?

3. Would/Could you turn down the volume?

H 1. might not want 2. might miss 3. might not pass

4. might not know

Unit 17

p. 112

Infinitives

Learn & Practice 1

A 1. to buy 2. to sleep 3. to take 4. to meet 5. to play

6. to watch 7. to study

Learn & Practice 2

A 1. me to finish 2. us to leave 3. me to write

4. you to join 5. him to drive 6. her to come

7. their neighbors to be

Learn & Practice 3

A 1. to 2. to 3. for 4. to 5. for

B 1. b 2. d 3. e 4. c 5. a

Super Writing

A 1. wants to go to Paris. She would like to see the Eiffel Tower.

2. wants to go to Egypt. He would like to see the Pyramids.

3. want to go to Korea. They would like to see the Seoul Tower.

4. wants to go to London. He would like to see Big Ben.

B 1. She went to the train station to catch a train.

2. She went to the library to return a book.

3. She went to a flower shop to buy some flowers.

4. She went to a coffee shop to meet a friend.

C 1. told Maria to stay at his house on Saturday night

2. advised me to see a doctor

3. told me to turn left after the bridge

4. ordered us to tidy the bedroom

5. invited us to come to her house for a barbecue on Saturday

6. persuaded Peter to wash his feet

D 1. She wants to lose weight to be the most beautiful at the party.

2. John went to France to learn French.

3. My sister is going shopping to buy some fresh fruit.

4. I stayed at home to help my mother.

5. I learn English to communicate with other people.

6. Cathy went to the store to buy a newspaper.

Learn & Practice 1

A 1. Watching TV
   2. Taking a good rest
   3. Learning a foreign language
   4. Reading in a dark room

Learn & Practice 2

A 1. playing 2. driving / to drive 3. doing / to do 4. to take 5. painting 6. to go 7. singing / to sing 8. opening

Learn & Practice 3

A 1. Would you like to go fishing?
   2. Would you like to go sailing?
   3. Would you like to go skating?
   4. Would you like to go sightseeing?
   5. Would you like to go shopping?

B 1. goes fishing 2. goes shopping 3. goes jogging
   4. go camping

Super Writing

A 1. Lucy likes playing the piano.
   2. Kathy enjoys listening to music.
   3. I put off doing my work.
   4. They enjoy baking and eating cupcakes.

B 1. Peter enjoys riding a bicycle.
   2. Peter can't stand waking up early.
   3. Peter hates brushing his teeth.
   4. Peter avoids fighting with his sister.
   5. Peter doesn't mind cleaning his room.
   6. Peter will stop playing computer games.

C 1. I hate doing my homework.
      I hate to do my homework.
   2. It began raining.
      It began to rain.
   3. He loves going to soccer games.
      He loves to go to soccer games.
   4. Nancy hates driving on city streets during rush hour.
      Nancy hates to drive on city streets during rush hour.

D 1. went swimming 2. go camping 3. went shopping

4. goes jogging
E 1. Climbing rocks is dangerous.
   2. Jogging every day is good for your health.
   3. Speaking in English is hard at first.
   4. Sleeping well is essential for health.

Learn & Practice 1

A 1. ✕ 2. to 3. ✕ 4. to 5. ✕ 6. ✕ 7. ✕ 8. to

Learn & Practice 2

A 1. Sara would like to go to the zoo.
   2. He would like a cup of coffee.
   3. She would like to have a cup of green tea.
   4. Mary would like some cheese on her pasta.
   5. We would like to make a snowman.
   6. They would like to go snowboarding.

B 1. Q: Would she like a bottle of mineral water?
      A: she would
   2. Q: Would he like to learn Japanese?
      A: he wouldn't
   3. Q: Would you like to have something to eat?
      A: I/we would
   4. Q: Would they like some dessert?
      A: they wouldn't
   5. Q: Would Jessica like to go to the movie theater?
      A: she would

Learn & Practice 3

A 1. doesn't like to watch
   2. would like to go
   3. doesn't like to study
   4. Would; like to come
   5. Does; like to do

Super Writing

A 1. She likes cars.
   2. He would like to go to Egypt for his next trip.
   3. She likes to dance. / She likes dancing..
   4. They would like to go to the zoo.
   5. Bob would like to become a professional singer one day.
   6. She likes spending her time at home. / She likes to

spend her time at home.

7. Why would you like to become a movie star?

C 1. I want to drink some water.

2. She needs a cup of coffee.

3. He needs to buy a new coat.

4. I want to play soccer with you.

5. I don't need a new car.

6. Lisa wants a salad with her pasta.

D 1. Would you like to go to the party tonight?

2. Would you like to play volleyball with me tomorrow?

3. Would you like to go to Korea with me next week?

4. Would you like to borrow my pen?

E 1. Would you like 2. Do you like 3. Would you like

4. Would you like 5. Do you like

Unit 20

Comparison

p. 130

1. F 2. T 3. F 4. T 5. F 6. T

Learn & Practice 1

A 1. cheaper 2. longer 3. harder

Learn & Practice 2

A 1. smaller 2. bigger 3. younger 4. more slowly

5. prettier 6. longer 7. hotter 8. thinner 9. easier

10. larger 11. older 12. faster 13. more quickly

14. harder 15. happier 16. more important

17. more difficult 18. cheaper 19. more famous

20. fatter 21. heavier

Learn & Practice 3

A 1. as old as 2. as tall as 3. as clean as 4. as cold as

5. as dangerous as 6. as big as

B 1. Sunny's sister isn't as pretty as Sunny.

2. I am not as old as you.

3. Bob isn't as tall as John.

4. I don't study as hard as her.

Super Writing

A 1. Steve is taller than Lisa.

2. Jessica's hair is longer than Daniel's hair.

3. The smartphone is more expensive than the MP3 player.

4. The rugby ball is bigger than the tennis ball.

5. The car is heavier than the bicycle.

6. Susan is thinner than her husband.

B 1. The papaya is as sweet as the mango.

2. My dog is as fierce as your dog.

3. The white dress is as expensive as the blue dress.

4. Jessica is as artistic as her sister.

5. Mark is as old as Linda.

C 1. A: Canada is bigger than China.

A: China is smaller than Canada.

2. A: The Nile is longer than the Han River.

A: The Han River is shorter than the Nile.

3. A: English is easier than Korean.

A: Korean is more difficult than English.

D 1. London is not as beautiful as Paris.

2. Nick isn't as heavy as George.

3. The earth isn't as big as the sun.

4. Peter doesn't speak as slowly as William.

E 1. as fast as Lisa

2. faster than Kathy

3. more carelessly than Scott

4. as hard as Alice

5. more clearly than Susan

Review Test (Unit 17-20)

p. 136

A 1. Eric likes planes. He wants to be a pilot.

2. Sunny likes animals. She wants to be a vet.

3. Jane likes movies. She wants to be an actress.

4. They like soccer. They want to be soccer players.

B 1. An ostrich is bigger than a penguin.

2. Gold is more expensive than silver.

3. Feathers are lighter then stones.

4. A car is faster than a bicycle.

C 1. to 2. for 3. to 4. for

D 1. They need to go to school.

2. He needs a wake-up call in the morning.

3. I need to relax for a while.

E 1. Tokyo is not as beautiful as Seoul.

2. Lisa isn't as heavy as Kevin.

3. The moon isn't as big as the earth.

4. Amy doesn't drive as slowly as Steve.

F 1. e 2. c 3. a 4. d 5. b 6. f

G 1. Would you like 2. would you like 3. do you like

4. Do you like

H **1.** go swimming **2.** go skiing **3.** going shopping
  4. go fishing
I **1.** She went to Chicago to visit her grandparents.
  2. She went to the bookstore to buy some books.
  3. They went to the travel agency to reserve a flight.